LINGUISTIC INTRODUCTION TO SANSKRIT

LINGUISTIC INTRODUCTION TO SANSKRIT

BATAKRISHNA GHOSH

GYAN

Published by

GYAN

Gyan Publishing House
5, Ansari Road
Daryaganj, New Delhi-110002
Phone: 011-47034999, 9811692060
E-mail: books@gyanbooks.com

Distribution Network
gyanbooks.com
India, USA, Canada, UK, Australia

ISBN: 978-93-6920-615-5 (HB)

First Published, 1937

2nd Impression 2025

Printed at: Gyan Press, Delhi.

LINGUISTIC INTRODUCTION TO SANSKRIT
Author: BATAKRISHNA GHOSH

INDIAN RESEARCH INSTITUTE PUBLICATIONS

Linguistic Series—No. 1

LINGUISTIC INTRODUCTION TO SANSKRIT

BY

BATAKRISHNA GHOSH

Dr. Phil. (Munich), D. Litt. (Paris),
Membre de la Société Asiatique de Paris,
Lecturer, University of Calcutta.

PUBLISHED BY

SATIS CHANDRA SEAL, M. A., B. L.

Hony. General Secretary

THE INDIAN RESEARCH INSTITUTE

170, MANIKTALA STREET

CALCUTTA

1937

BY THE SAME AUTHOR :–

1. Hindu Law and Custom
   (Authorised English translation of Jolly's *Recht und Sitte*), Calcutta 1928.
2. Les Formations Nominales et Verbales en p du Sanskrit, Paris 1933.
3. Collection of Fragments of Lost Brāhmaṇas, Calcutta 1935.
4. Jaiminiya Brāhmaṇa (text, translation and notes)
   (shortly to be out)
5. Pāli Literature and Language
   (shortly to be out—authorised English translation of Geiger's *Pāli Literatur und Sprache*).

INSCRIBED

TO THE MEMORY OF

MY GRAND-FATHER

PANDIT KEDARNATH GHOSH

A NOTE

The Indian Research Institute has much pleasure to present before the scholarly world the first publication of its Linguistic Series—"Linguistic Introduction to Sanskrit" by Dr. Batakrishna Ghosh, Dr. Phil. (Munich), D. Litt. (Paris). The publication of a treatise such as this was a desideratum and Dr. Ghosh now removes this long-felt want.

The only linguistic grammar of the Sanskrit Language is Wackernagel's "Altindische Grammatik", three volumes of which are still to appear. But even the volumes which we have before us are not such as can be easily understood by our students. The author of this book will consider his labour amply repaid if it can prepare our students for Wackernagel's great work.

We have every hope that this short treatise will be a very useful guide to students of Vedic Sanskrit and Comparative Philology and that this new publication will evoke the same warm response from all lovers of Indology as our other previous publications.

Dated, the 1st January 1937.
The Indian Research Institute
Calcutta.

Satis Chandra Seal.

PREFACE

In the following little book I have tried to present as clearly as possible what I think our University students can and should know of Vedic Sanskrit and Comparative Philology, and in this venture I have been largely guided by my teaching experience at the Universities of Dacca and Calcutta. At present in India the mediaeval commentaries are taught in the name of the Vedas and hardly any attention is paid to the texts themselves. The students leaving the University therefore usually go away with the idea that the Vedic Ṛṣis were either ignorant of grammar or did not care to follow its rules. I have tried to show in this book how much more complex than Pāṇini's was the grammar followed by the Ṛṣis, and how much we have to depend on the evidence of other cognate languages for an adequate comprehension of the forms and structure of the Vedic language. Students of Comparative Philology will find in this book, I hope, a dependable guide to the science through the medium of the Sanskrit language.

If the twentieth century has brought any new idea to the science of linguistics, it is, I believe, that language is not a mere vocal substitute for ink and paper to communicate to others our thoughts and sensations. Language, we are beginning to realise, is above all a picture of the mind, and its ways are determined more by phonetic *limitations* than by phonetic *laws*. Within the boundaries set by these limitations the mind acts as a free agent, and language is *created* every time the conscious mind speaks. The battle-cry of "Ausnahmslosigkeit" can but evoke a smile to-day, for it can not even explain our phonology and not at all our syntax. But to build up a system of comparative phonology solely, or mainly, on the principle of phonetic limitations is a task attended with insuperable difficulties. I had therefore no other choice but to adhere to the tradition created by the Junggrammatiker, later but slightly modified. On one point of principle however I have dared to differ,—or at least to clearly indicate that I do so. I do not believe that a living organism that the language is can be dissected into convenient morsels and still retain its original character. Linguistic grammars divided into water-tight compartments such as phonology, morphology, syntax, therefore cannot but be misleading. For concatenation of internal problems is one of the chief signs of life in which also the language participates. Could I have my way, I would begin with the bases and derive from them phonology on the one hand and morphology on the other. But that would be too radical a departure, unsuited to a "Linguistic Introduction".

In writing this book I often missed the guiding instructions of my honoured teachers Professors Wüst (Munich) and Renou (Paris). Had it been possible for me to consult them on the many points that I would have liked to, this book would have been surely much less imperfect than it is. Yet my debt to them is such that it is not mere courtesy which impels me to say, whatever good there may be in this book is due to them and all the faults are mine. To Professor Wackernagel I am deeply indebted for the great interest he evinced in my work. After seeing some portion of this work he wrote to me, "Ihre Arbeit bringt etwas ganz Neues nach Indien und macht eigentlich Epoche." Such warm praise from such high authority was indeed beyond my expectation. I can think of no higher recompense than that the book now completed might evoke the same warm approval from this greatest living linguist and Sanskritist. To Professors Suniti Kumar Chatterji (Calcutta), Prabadh Chandra Bagchi (Calcutta) and Sushil Kumar De (Dacca) I am indebted not only for constant encouragement but also for lending me books out of their personal libraries. Lastly I place on record my deep gratitude to the Indian Research Institute, for taking up this book as the first number of its Linguistic Series.

CONTENTS

INDO-EUROPEAN ORIGIN OF SANSKRIT.

Some of the most important languages, living or dead, known to us are now generally grouped under the designation Indo-European. A great deal of uselsss controversy has raged over the designation to be attached to this group, but it has never been contested that the languages regarded as belonging to this group are characterised by a large number of common peculiar features. The linguists are prepared to go even one step further and state in categorical terms what in their opinion is the only possible explanation of these common peculiar features in such a large number of languages. They will say that however different these languages may appear to be they are essentially continuations of one and the same idiom under different circumstances, for the existence of which however no direct evidence is available. The cause of this differentiation is to be sought not only in the external aspects of life such as time and climate ; it may be inherent also in the subject speaking the language. Even under identical conditions of life two different persons cannot speak the identical language. For language is one of the forms of expression of life, however imperfect in this case, and it reflects the mind of the individual as determined by heredity and modified by experience. The same forms of speech evoked from different persons by the same circumstances symbolise as often as not emotions and sensations altogether different, and where this difference is sufficiently pronounced it may find expression also in the language. It is clear therefore that the hypothetical original idiom from which the various Indo-European dialects are supposed to have originated, cannot but be a fiction. In fact neither is it claimed by modern linguists. The original Indo-European, as this hypothetical language is called, is but a convenient formula to cover an *ensemble* of individual idioms all slightly differing from each other, spoken by the individual members of the ancient Indo-European community. These individual idioms mark the first stage of disintegration of the original Indo-European, and subject to the laws of the growth of languages, which favour the development of certain tendencies into distinct types and make the rest conform to them, they gradually gave rise to the great Indo-European dialects of the historical age. It is proved to-day that definite dialect-groups were formed among the ancient Indo-Europeans even before their general dispersal had begun.

The known Indo-European dialects may be conveniently divided into the following groups: (1) Indian (the most ancient Indian language of the Indo-European family being Sanskrit), (2) Iranian, (3) Armenian, (4) Albanian, (5) Slavic, (6) Baltic, (7) Greek, (8) Italic, (9) Celtic, (10) Germanic, to which now must be added (11) Tocharian and (12) Hittite. All these languages are marked by certain common characteristics which distinguish them from the other languages of the world. But already at the dawn of history the difference between them was very great and some of these languages had changed so much that even for the modern linguists it was not easy to recognise their Indo-European character. The entire science of comparative grammar of the Indo-European languages has grown out of the study of the points of difference and similarity existing between them, in the light of which the history and development of every individual dialect is to be traced. Such a comparative study is at all possible however because although every language changes and develops in its own way, it always follows definite laws. Otherwise it would not be possible to trace the history and development of any language in the world. Comparison between the isolated facts of particular languages would signify little or nothing at all had they not been symbols for entire systems of facts in these respective languages. Thus the parallelism between Skt. *ábharan* and Gr. *épheron* would have remained a mere linguistic curio without any scientific value if it could not be proved that every point of difference between these two forms is paralleled by a vast number of similar instances in these two languages, or, in other words, that they are due to certain particular tendencies by which these languages are characterised. We know, for instance, that for every Greek *e* Sanskrit has an *a* and for every Sanskrit *bh* Greek has a *ph*. Once these particular tendencies (or laws) which account for the difference between these two forms are accurately defined it is possible to give an explanation also of their similarity which is much more striking in this case. In other words, it is now possible to postulate the approximate original form which resulted in Skt. *ábharan* on the one hand and Greek *épheron* on the other under the influence of the divergent tendencies inherent in these languages. Thus it is customary to say that the original Indo-European proto-type of these forms was **ébheront*.

A large number of similar examples of correspondence between Sanskrit and Greek may be adduced to prove their common origin. In the same way a similar relation can be established between Sanskrit and every one of the other Indo-European dialects. But the correspondence is not equally clear in every case, for the laws of diverging tendencies cannot be defined with the same precision for all the languages and even in those cases where they can be defined with tolerable precision their normal action is often disturbed by analogy. Moreover, due to contact with foreign peoples, in every Indo-European dialect a large portion of the vocabulary was replaced by foreign loan-words and sometimes the entire phonetic structure of the language was changed. Thus the number of Semitic loan-words in Hittite and modern Persian is actually greater than that of words of Indo-European origin and there is reason to believe that the phonetic structure of Armenian is largely determined by the influence of the neighbouring Caucasian dialects, which however left its grammatical structure untouched. It is impossible to say whether the consonant shift of the Germanic languages is due to a similar cause, but it can be hardly doubted that the rise of the cerebral series in Sanskrit was possible only because of contact with Munda and Dravidian languages (we will have occasion to speak at greater length on this controversial point). In almost all the modern Indo-European dialects the accent has become predominantly expiratory to-day, although it is quite certain that the original Indo-European accent was predominantly musical. This fundamental change in the nature of accent had far-reaching effects on the development of Indo-European dialects, for it entailed the weakening of vowels in unstressed syllables as in Latin and loss of final syllables as in Germanic and Celtic.

Herein also lies one of the fundamental differences between Sanskrit and Prākrit. The original Indo-European was a strictly flexional language, so that the sentence in Indo-European dialects was composed of independent units. Every word conveyed not only a complete thought-content but also expressed its relation with other parts of the sentence. But even this, one of the chief characteristics of the original Indo-European, is gradually disappearing from the modern Indo-European dialects, and modern English or Persian is more isolating than flexional in character. For in them the interrelation between different parts of the sentence is expressed not by flexional endings but by position and particles.

Due to all these and various other multifarious causes every one of the Indo-European dialects has changed almost beyond recognition and it is possible to establish their common origin to-day only with the help of the science of Comparative Grammar. Already at the dawn of history the process of divergence had advanced so far that the civilised peoples of those days speaking Indo-European dialects, although in constant contact with each other, never suspected that their respective languages are derived from one original idiom. Eminent Greek savants and politicians lived at the Persian Court, many of them had even mastered the Persian language, but to all of them it was merely a barbaric speech. Yet, even across the great gulf of time and space, every Indo-European dialect has retained many essential features of the original Indo-European in phonetic structure, morphology, syntax and vocabulary, and none more than Sanskrit.

Perhaps the most characteristic feature of Indo-European phonetics is its three series of gutturals. The gutturals in our own dialect too are far from homogeneous in character, for the *k* in *ki*, *ka* and *ku* is fundamentally different in each case. The *k* in *ki* is very much like *c*, and in *ku* it is hardly distinguishable from the sound *kw*. The *k* in *ka* holds an intermediate position. The closure takes place in each case at a different place : in *ki* high on the palate, in *ka* on the soft palate (velum) and in *ku* still lower on the velum with a concomitant rounding of the lips. According to these organs of articulation these gutturals are called palatal, velar and labio-velar respectively and three different signs are used in comparative grammar to indicate them, viz., $\hat{k}$, q and q^{u}. In our own dialect, as usually in all other languages, the character of the guttural is largely determined by the following vowel. It will be palatal when it is followed by a palatal vowel like *i* or *e*, and it will be velar when it is followed by a lower vowel like *a* or *u*. But the special feature of the original Indo-European consists in that it seems to have allowed gutturals of every kind in any position irrespective of the following vowel. This is what is meant when it is said that the original Indo-European possessed three series of gutturals. Thus it appears that our Indo-European forefathers could easily pronounce a labio-velar q^{u} even when the following vowel was *i* or *e*, and a palatal $\hat{k}$ even when it was followed by *o* or *u*. Their linguistic descendants all over the world find it however very difficult to-day to pronounce such sound-combinations.

The three series of gutturals postulated for the original Indo-European cannot however be found in any Indo-European dialect known to us. The pure velars have proved to be a very unstable element in the Indo-European guttural system, for in one section of these dialects they have been completely merged in the palatals and in another in the labio-velars. The treatment of the Indo-European palatal is singularly different in these two sections. In one group it remains a true occlusive, but in the other it becomes a spirantic sibilant. Thus the original Indo-European word for 'hundred' was **k̂m̥tóm* with an initial palatal occlusive. But the form derived from it in Sanskrit is *śatám*, in Avestan *satəm*, in Old Church Slavic *sŭto*, in Lithuanian *szimtas*, etc.—each beginning with a sibilant. On the other hand, in another group of Indo-European dialects the word for 'hundred' begins with a guttural occlusive, cf. Greak (*he-*) *katón*, Latin *centum*, Old Irish *cét*, Tocharian *kant*, etc. The Indo-European dialects are therefore divided into two distinct groups so far as the treatment of the original palatal series is concerned. For the sake of convenience the first group is called *Satəm* and the second *Centum* after the words for 'hundred' in Avestan and Latin respectively. In the *Satəm* group the pure velars coincide with the labiovelars and in the *Centum* group they coincide with the palatals.[1] The question now naturally arises, how to know where we have to do with a pure velar if there is no direct independent evidence about its existence in any known Indo-European dialect. Thus if a word occurs only in the *Satəm* languages, such as Skt. *kṛṣṇá*, O. Ch. Sl. *črĭnŭ*, etc., it is impossible to say whether the initial consonant was a pure velar or a labio-velar, and in the case of words occurring only in the *Centum* languages, such as Gr. *kephalḗ*, O. H.

1. Some eminent linguists are inclined to doubt the independent existence of pure velars in the original Indo-European. Without ignoring this possibility we shall here adhere to the usual terminology.

G. *gebal* etc., it is impossible to say whether the initial consonant was a palatal or a pure velar. But an original pure velar can be easily detected by the process of elimination if the word concerned occurs both in the *Centum* and the *Satəm* groups. In fact, if a word shows a pure velar both in its *Satəm* and *Centum* forms a pure velar may be postulated also for its original Indo-European form. If palatal, it would have become a sibilant in the *Satəm* languages, and if labio-velar, of the *Centum* languages in Greek it would have become a dental or a labial (cf. Gr. *téttares* : Lith. *keturi* and Gr. *poinè* : Av. *kaēnā*) and in Latin and Germanic it would have been pronounced with a rounding of the lips (cf. Lat. *quis*, Goth. *his* : Skt. (*na*)*kis*). Thus forms like Skt. *kravis*, Gr. *kréas*, Lat. *cruor*, etc. prove that the initial consonant in the original Indo-European form of the word was a pure velar.[1] Only in those cases where the guttural in question is followed by *u* is it impossible to determine its original character even though the word containing it occurs both in *Satəm* and *Centum* languages, for an original labio-velar followed by *u* is pronounced without the rounding of lips even in the *Centum* languages (in the *Satəm* languages the original labio-velar is under no circumstances pronounced with the rounding of lips). In Skt. *kūpa* : Gr. *kúpē*, Lat. *cūpa*, for instance, it is impossible to say whether the initial guttural was originally a velar or a labio-velar. Thus, unusual though it may appear, three different types of gutturals,

1. It must be admitted however that the special character of the sounds in the neighbourhood of the pure velar in this and the few other instances considerably weakens the argument for its independent existence in the original Indo-European.

irrespective of the vowels following them, seem to have actually existed in the original Indo-European, and the colourful history of their later development can be followed in no other single Indo-European dialect better than in Sanskrit. On the other hand we shall see that the various subtle phonetic phenomena concealed behind the familiar forms of Sanskrit gutturals and palatals can be discovered only with the help of sister Indo-European dialects.

Another peculiar feature of the Indo-European sound system is its four categories of occlusives, namely surd, surd aspirate, sonant and sonant aspirate. Every series of occlusives,—guttural, dental or labial—, was composed of four distinct sounds of the above description. The entire system of Indo-European occlusives may therefore be tabulated in the following way :—

	Surd.	Surd asp.	Son.	Son. asp.
Gutturals	$\hat{k}$	$\hat{k}h$	$\hat{g}$	$\hat{g}h$
	q	qh	g	gh
	q^{u}	$q^{u}h$	g^{u}	$g^{u}h$
Dentals	t	th	d	dh
Labials	p	ph	b	bh

All these various sounds occurred with very different frequency in the original Indo-European. The sonant aspirates, for instance, were much more frequent than the surd aspirates or the pure sonants. It is therefore surprising to see that Sanskrit is the only Indo-European dialect which has preserved these original sonant aspirates (in the modern Indo-Aryan dialects they have become more or less spirantic along with the surd aspirates). In the other dialects they have either become surd aspirates as in Greek or pure sonants as in Iranian, Germanic and the Balto-slavic languages, or various spirantic sounds have been developed out of them as in Latin and Celtic. Thus to Skt. *bhárāmi* corresponds Gr. *phérō*, Goth. *bairo* and Lat. *fero*. The original sonant aspirate is not always quite apparent from the corresponding forms in the Indo-European dialects, for in Sanskrit and Greek, the only two languages which have preserved the original aspiration, two aspitrates are never allowed either in one and the same syllable, or at the beginning of two successive syllables in the same word. In all such cases one of the two aspirates, generally the preceding one, is changed into a pure surd or sonant as the case may be, through dissimilation. Thus the original form of the Sanskrit root *dah-* was **dhagh-*, with two sonant aspirates, which however never appear together in any flexional form of this root. Generally the initial consonant drops its aspiration in favour of that of the final (cf. *dáh-a-ti*, *dah-yá-te*, etc.) and that is how the ancient Indian grammarians were led to believe that the real form of the root was *dah-*. But whenever the final sonant aspirate is compelled to drop its aspiration the initial consonant at once avails itself of the opportunity and appears in its original aspirated form (cf. *á-dhāk*, *á-dhāk-ṣ-it*, etc.). There are some exceptions to this rule in the older language in the case of flexional ending with aspirates (cf. *da-dhā́-the*, *dhe-hí*, etc.), but they are mostly due to analogy (thus the irregular form *da-dhā́-the* is visibly due to the analogical influence of *da-dhā́-te*) or are purposely resorted to for the sake of obtaining clear and unambiguous forms (thus the regular form of *dhā-* in 2. sg. Impv. act. ought to have been **de-hí* and not *dhe-hí*, but then it could not have been distinguished from the similar form of *dā-*). Very remarkable however is the case of nominal flexional endings with *bh-*, in whose case the law of dissimilation of aspirates is never observed (forms like *bhūbhyā́m, dhī-bhis, asthá-bhyas* are quite normal), perhaps because these endings were joined to the stem at a later date. It is to be noticed that in the *Padapāṭha* these endings are regularly separated from the stem. Now the same law of dissimilation of aspirates is seen also in Greek. The original stem-form of the word for hair in Greek was *thrich-*, but the two aspirates alternate with each other in the various flexional forms of this stem, cf. *thríx* but *trichós*. The verb *échō* is etymologically connected with Skt. *sah-* and therefore the initial vowel should have had spiritus asper. That it shows spiritus lenis instead is due to the fact that it is followed by the aspirate *ch*. But whenever this *ch* drops its aspiration on account of combination with *s* the initial vowel shows spiritus asper, cf. *héxō*. As in Sanskrit, so in Greek too, the action of this law is sometimes disturbed through analogy, cf. *sóthē-thi* instead of **sótē-thi* through the influence of forms like *sōthḗtō*, etc. Due to the effect of this law in Sanskrit and Greek the same original root sometimes assumes very different forms in these two languages. Thus the Indo-European root *bheudh-* has given rise to forms like *bódh-a-ti, búdh-ya-te,* etc. in Sanskrit (root *budh-*, cf. however *bhot-syá-ti*), but in Greek the corresponding forms are *peúth-o-mai, punth-á-no-mai*, etc. In the same way the Indo-European root *bhendh-* has given rise to Sanskrit *badh-nā́-mi, ba-bándh-a* etc. (root *bandh-*, cf. however *bhant-syá-ti*), but in Greek it appears in the form *penth-* in *pentherós* 'father-in-law' (cf. *bandhu* 'relation' in Sanskrit, derived from the same root). In Latin it has assumed the form *fend-*

(cf. *of-fend-ix*) and in Germanic the vowel *e*—further became *i* before the covered nasal and gave rise to the corresponding Germanic root *bind-*.

It will appear from above that the Indo-European consonant system was very faithfully preserved in Sanskrit, but the Indo-European vowel-system was completely changed in it. Yet even in this respect Sanskrit has preserved some archaic features for which we look in vain in the other dialects. A peculiar feature of the Indo-European vowel-system is its syllabic liquids. Excepting in some Slavic dialects these syllabic liquids have been given up in all other Indo-European languages, but syllabic *r* (ṛ) is quite common in Sanskrit and the syllabic *l* (ḷ) occurs at least in the root *kḷp-*. The quantity of Avestan vowels being very uncertain the existence of long diphthongs in the original Indo-European could not have been proved without the help of Sanskrit. All Indo-European short diphthongs have become monophthongs in Sanskrit; thus, for instance, I.-E. **ei-ti*, Lith. *eĩti* but Skt. *éti*; I.-E. **bheudh-e-ti*, Gr, *peúth-o-mai* but Skt. *bódh-a-ti*. Indo-European long diphthongs how ever are still real diphthongs in Sanskrit, but they have retained their original character only by sacrificing the length of their first components. Thus Sanskrit goes with all the other dialects in making the long diphthongs short, but on account of its differential treatment of the short diphthongs it betrays the existence of long diphthongs in the original Indo-European. That all Sanskrit diphthongs were originally long is proved by the fact that *ai au* before a consonant usually corresponds to *āy āv* before a vowel, cf. *gaú-s*: *gā́v-am*, *nau-bhís*: *nā́v-am*, etc., and whenever a final diphthong is dissolved through sandhi its first component is observed to be invariably long. Yet it is quite certain that already in the earliest Sanskrit these diphthongs had become short, for the RV. shows forms like *praiṣayúr* (RV. I, 120, 5) composed of *prá* and *iṣayúr*, and from the data of the Prātiśākhyas it is clear that there was a strong tendency to pronounce the diphthong *ai* as *ayi*. From the stand-point of Sanskrit it is therefore incorrect and often misleading to transcribe Sanskrit diphthongs by *āi āu* as is done by many Sanskritists even to this day. Moreover, such an historical system of transcription would demand *ei eu* etc. in the place of Sanskrit *e o*.

Passing on to Indo-European morphology we shall see that in this field too Sanskrit continues the old Indo-European tradition more faithfully than any other Indo-European dialect, but we shall also see that most of the various forms in Sanskrit cannot be fully comprehended without comparison with other dialects. The Indo-European system of nominal declension expressed, firstly, the relation between the substantive and the verb, or, more rarely, that between one substantive and another (e. g. in genitive), and secondly, the numerical quality of the substantive in question. Thus from the first point of view the declensional forms can be divided into eight groups of so-called *cases*, namely nominative, accusative, instrumental, dative, ablative, genitive, locative and vocative (in the order followed in Sanskrit), and from the second the three *numbers*,—singular, dual and plural. Sanskrit alone has preserved intact all these eight cases and three numbers, in all the other dialects the highly complex Indo-European system of nominal declension has been variously simplified. For the eight different cases Sanskrit has however only three different forms in the dual (one for nom., acc. and voc., one for instr., dat. and abl., and one for gen. and loc.). This shows that even in Sanskrit the dual was subjected to that process of simplification which resulted in its complete disappearance from many of the Indo-European dialects. In Latin, for instance, the dual does not exist at all as a grammatical category and in Greek declension only two forms are met with in dual. In Lithuanian and Old Church Slavic too the variety of forms in dual is considerably restricted and in Gothic it is to be found only in the pronominal declension. The same tendency towards simplification may be observed also in the use of cases. Leaving the vocative out of consideration, Sanskrit has the full set of seven distinct cases, Lithuanian and Old Church Slavic six, Latin five, Greek and Gothic only four. The functions of the original seven cases were thus distributed among much fewer ones in the various other dialects and in the process even the case-suffixes had to be transferred from one case to another. Thus though the ablative singular ending of *e/o*-stems in Latin is derived from the corresponding ending in the original Indo-European, the ablative plural ending *-īs* is but the continuation of the I.-E. Instr. plur. ending *-ois*. And it is well known that the Latin ablative combines in itself also the function of the original instrumental. But though in Latin the ablative holds such an important position it is to be noted that excepting in it and Sanskrit it has survived in no other language. In fact even in the original Indo-European the formal existence of the ablative as an independent case was rather precarious. In dual and plural it was never distinguished from the dative and in singular it was distinguished from the genitive only in the case of *e/o*-stems.

In the Indo-European system of declension the accent was sometimes on the stem and sometimes on the ending. The stem shows a fuller form where it bore the accent in the original Indo-European, though it may have shifted position in the known Indo-European dialects, and it shows a reduced form where the original accent stood on the ending. In the technical language of the science of linguistics these fuller case-forms are called strong and the reduced forms are called weak. It is curious to note that the distribution of strong and weak case-forms is exactly the same in Sanskrit and Greek—the only two languages in which the subtle action of accent can be best studied. This gradation of stem in the nominal flexion did not escape the eye of Pāṇini who designated the strong forms by the technical term *sarvanāmasthāna* but understood by it only the first five forms in Sanskrit declension. Modern linguistics would include in this category also the locative (and the vocative) of singular. In the declension of *pitár*, for instance, the stem in the strong forms is *pitar-* (the form *pitā́* in nom. sg. is due to a special cause) and in the weak forms it is *pitr-* or *pitṛ-* according as it is followed by a vowel or a consonant, and in Greek the corresponding strong form of the stem is *pater-* and its weak form is *patr-* or *patra-* according to the nature of the following sound. Thus for Skt. strong forms *pitā́, pitár-au, pitár-i* we find in Greek *patḗr, patér-e, patér-i* (original loc. become dat. in Greek), and for the Skt. weak form *pitṛ́-ṣu* we have an exact parallel in Gr. *patrá-si*. The original state of things has been greatly disturbed both in Sanskrit and Greek, so that analogous forms do not always correspond to each other in them. Moreover there is reason to believe that in some cases at least the strong form was extended also to other positions already in the original Indo-European.

Coming to the endings themselves, it is necessary only to cast a glance on the corresponding inflexion-systems of the various Indo-European dialects to be convinced that they are variations of one original prototype. Everywhere we find an *-s* in nom. sg., an *-m* in acc. sg., an *-ōm* in gen. pl., etc. Apart from isolated cases in particular languages there is real difficulty only in conciliating the consonantal endings with *bh-* in Sanskrit with the corresponding endings in some of the other dialects. From the stand-point of these endings the Indo-European dialects may be divided into two groups as from the stand-point of Indo-European gutturals, but the groups thus formed do not by any means coincide with each other. The endings in one group of dialects, including Sanskrit, Armenian and Latin, seem to be derived from forms characterised by a *bh-* (cf. Skt.*-bhyas*: Lat.*-bus*) whereas in another group, including the Balto-Slavic and the Germanic languages, the corresponding endings are characterised by an *-m* instead (cf. Lith.*-mus*, Old Ch. Sl. *-mŭ*, Goth.*-m* in dat. pl.). Thus in each of the *bh-* and *m-* groups are included both *Centum* and *Satəm* languages. The ending *-phi* or *-phin* in Homeric Greek, which seems to have been used indiscriminately for all cases and numbers, is a precious relic in Greek of the *bh*-endings. Yet however the distinction is not always clear between these two *bh-* and *m*-groups, for though O. Ch. Sl. belongs to the *m*-group, its *tebja* (2. pron. dat. sg.) exactly corresponds to Latin *tibi*, whose ending is evidently derived from a *bh*-form. Such anomalous forms naturally suggest a probable clue to the original distribution of *bh-* and *m*-endings. Perhaps the *bh*-endings were originally associated with pronouns alone and the *m*-endings with the nouns, but later through analogy in certain languages the *bh*-endings were generalised also for the nouns and in others the *m*-endings almost wholly dispossessed the *bh*-endings of their own dominion. Be that as it may, in Sanskrit every *bh*-ending seems to be a combination of *bhi* with some other element : *-bhis* in Instr. pl. seems to be nothing but this *bhi* augmented by an *s* which characterises every plural case-form excepting the genitive. In the dual ending *-bhyām* the same *bhi* is augmented by *-ām*, certainly connected with the *-am* which plays such an important part in Sanskrit pronominal inflexion (cf. Lat. *tibi* : Skt. *túbhy-am*, Lat. *mihi* : Skt. *máhy-am*), and in the plural ending *-bhyas* it is augmented by *-a(s)*. Now if these augment elements are left aside as later adjuncts we get also for Sanskrit, just as in Homeric Greek, an ending *-bhi* which was used indiscriminately for various cases and numbers. Moreover it is to be noticed in this connection that the *bh*-ending in Sanskrit, both in dual and in plural, evince a peculiar tendency to repeat themselves. Various other 'anomalies' of Sanskrit inflexion would appear to date from the hoary antiquity if the other Indo-European dialects are compared. The ending *-āsas* in nom. pl. of *e/o*-stems in Vedic has been for long a puzzle to linguists, but the genial explanation given by Meillet is now generally accepted. According to M. this double ending was resorted to in Vedic in the case of e/o-stems in order to make the number of syllables in the nom. pl. of these stems conform to that of similar forms of other stems. *e/o*-stems were always regarded as the norm of Indo-European declensional

2

stems, but M. proved that *i* and *u*-stems (I.-E. *ei eu*-stems) have a better claim to be regarded as such, for the disyllabic *devā́s* was changed into the trisyllabic *devā́sas* in analogy with the trisyllabic *áhayas* (from *áhi*) etc. Now it is really surprising that the double ending in the nom. pl. of *e/o*-stems seems to be of Indo-European antiquity, for the Old English form *dómas* (stem. *dóm*) in nom. pl. can be satisfactorily explained in terms of the phonetic laws obtaining in Germanic languages entailing the loss of final syllables only if it is assumed that the original ending had been a double one.

The most difficult chapter in the Sanskrit Grammar is decidedly that on the verb. It is mostly in connection with the verbal system that the ancient Indian grammarians failed to render a faithful account of the Vedas, for they missed the fundamental point that the vast multitude of forms making up the Sanskrit verbal system is divided in the first line according to moods into the forms of indicative, injunctive, subjunctive, optative and imperative. This mistake was also natural, for in the days of classical Sanskrit, when these grammars were written, the original verbal system had been greatly simplified. But even the Vedic verbal system offers but a very incomplete picture of the original Indo-European verbal system. To begin with, we shall have to be prepared to admit that the Indo-European verbal system was essentially of a non-temporal character, that is to say, every verb-form expressed rather the *how* than the *when* of a particular action. Excepting the use of the preverb *e* to indicate past action, which appears as augment in the augment-tenses of Sanskrit, Avestan, Armenian and Greek, there was to all appearance nothing in the Indo-European verbal system to express the temporal quality of the action concerned. The perfect stem of a verbal root, for instance, does not signify a past completed action but expresses a certain condition of the subject resulting from a previous action. The perfect form *véda* signifies that the subject has discovered a certain thing and therefore knows it thoroughly. Similarly *dādhāra* from *dhar-* signifies that the subject is on the way to get hold of a certain thing as the result of some previous action. Thus *yát sāyám juhóti rátryai téna dādhāra* signifies "in that he makes offering in the evening he secures (Agni) for the night". There is not the slightest suggestion of a past tense here. The perfect has exactly the same function in Homeric Greek, though in the oldest Latin and Germanic the perfect shows a fully developed temporal meaning. The difference between the persent and the aorist too lay originally only in the manner of action and the future was hardly distinguished from the subjunctive, a fact which explains why the future of Latin third and fourth conjugations is derived from the Indo-European subjunctive. From all this it would appear that our Indo-European fore-fathers had not yet learnt to think beyond the present when the general dispersal of their tribes began. With the growth of civilisation their descendants learnt to discriminate between past, present and future, but to express the new ideas they had at their disposal only the older forms whose function was altogether different. Hence the almost insuperable difficulty in the way of reconstructing anything like a complete picture of the Indo-European verbal system.

Yet what we can infer about it clearly shows that the Indo-European verbal system was fundamentally different from the verbal system of classical Sanskrit, Greek or any other Indo-European dialect. From the school grammars of these languages, it would appear that the bare mention of a particular root is enough to develop and set forth in all its details the complete verbal system, but an historical study of these languages will soon dispel this idea. It will show that almost every root has its own special features, that by no means are all the roots susceptible of all the voices, moods and tenses, and that according to the manner of action (*aspect*) the root had to assume special forms, though in the later dialects the variety of forms has been greatly simplified. A glance at Whitney's "Roots" will show that a wide gulf separates the actual language from the language of the grammars. If the above interpretation of the perfect is true, as it is generally considered to be, it must have been originally confined to verbs denoting some sort of continued action, and as the original function of the aorist was to express momentary action as opposed to durative, only verbs of the type *find* (as opposed to *see*) were originally eligible to aorist forms. Due to later confusion it is equally difficult to distinguish between the various original modal and temporal stems. We are familiar with subjunctives with long vowels in Sanskrit and Greek, but traces of short-vowel forms at their side are still abundant in these languages both in present and in aorist. Thus we have for present Skt. *kr̥ṇávat*(*i*) (ind. *kr̥ṇóti*) and Homeric *íomen* (ind. *í-men*), and for aorist Skt. *néšat*(*i*) (ind. *á-naiṣ-am*) and Homeric *teíso-men* (ind. *é-teis-a*). These short-vowel subjunctive forms however were gradually supplanted by the long-vowel ones, evidently because they were less ambiguous from the formantic point of view. Among the temporal stems sometimes the very same form functions in two very different capacities. Thus Skt. *ábhāt* is imperfect, but *ásthāt* is aorist. Again the corresponding Greek forms *éphē* (impf.) and *éstē* (aor.) prove that the line of demarcation between these two categories had been destroyed in this case already in the Indo-European epoch. The perfect stem has been on the whole handed down in its pure form, for it was distinguished from the beginning not only by partial reduplication but also by peculiar personal endings. It is all the more curious to note, therefore, that in most languages the function of the perfect stem has been taken up by other stems—in Latin and O. Ch. Sl. it has been largely supplanted by the aorist stem. Of the numerous modal and temporal stems of the original Indo-European verbal system the individual Indo-European dialects have retained only very few. In classical Sanskrit the aggregate of forms comprised in the entire system had become so limited that the Indian grammarians failed even to distinguish properly between the different moods. By a careful study of the Vedic forms and through comparison with other Indo-European dialects however much of the older verbal system can be still reconstructed. Thus through comparison can it be detected that Sanskrit has altogether shaken off the thematic ending *-o* in 1. person sg. just as Latin has done away with the athematic ending *-mi*. In Greek however both forms are living, and English *am* and German *bin* are lingering traces of the ending *-mi* in Germanic.

The science of comparative grammar has not yet succeeded in tackling with syntax with the same precision and on an equally broad basis as phonology and morphology. Yet the comparative study of the allied Indo-European dialects has thrown a flood of light on many of the most interesting syntactical peculiarities of Sanskrit. In the RV. several times a singular verb-form has been used in connection with a plural neuter substantive. This apparent anomaly could never have been explained without the help of Greek syntax which teaches that the plural neuter substantive shall always take a verb in the singular. Indeed the nom. pl. of neuter was itself often a singular even morphologically. The nom. pl. of *yugám* was *yugā́* (cf. Gr. *zúga*) which signified a plurality of yokes, not however in the distributive but in the collective sense. The ending in *yugā́* is evidently the same as in the nom. sg. of feminine *ā*-stems. In this way the use of singular verb-forms in connection with plural neuter substantives receives its natural and obvious explanation. The use of the fem. ending -*ā* to signify a collection of objects is a peculiar characteristic of the Indo-European dialects; cf. Gr. *mēroí*, but *mēra* when the plural has a collective sense, similarly Latin *loci* and *loca*. Enclitic pronouns exhibit a pronounced tendency in Sanskrit to occupy the second place in the sentence, even though it may thus give rise to ambiguity. Thus from *né 'n me 'gnír vaiśvānaró múkhān niṣpadyā́tai* it may appear that the enclitic *me* is connected with *agní* and that the whole sentence signifies "so that my Agni Vaiśvānara may not fall out of the mouth". In fact however *me* is connected with *múkhāt* and the purport of the sentence is, "so that A.V. may not fall out of my mouth". No satisfactory explanation of this astonishing tendency of the enclitica to occupy the second place can be given, but Wackernagel has proved that this peculiarity is shared also by Greek and other Indo-European dialects. The sentence quoted above betrays another syntactical peculiarity of Sanskrit. The verb in the principal sentence generally remains unaccented, but it is accented in the subordinate clause, and the preverb is often detached in the principal sentence but is always compounded in the subordinate clause. Nothing exactly parallel can be pointed out in the other allied dialects but there is ample indication to prove that the tendency to treat the finite verb as enclitic was present already in the original Indo-European. Thus in Greek the verb is unaccented after negations and other adverbs (preverbs including the augment), cf. *oú phēmi, prós labe* etc. Modern German offers a striking parallel to Sanskrit by assigning not only a special position but also a special accent to the finite verb in the subordinate clause. The Germanic form *sind* is but a later variation of I.-E. **sénti*, but its sonant *d* shows that the form from which it is directly derived must have been accentless.

Lastly also in vocabulary Sanskrit bears the stamp of the original Indo-European. A large number of parallel forms of Sanskrit words in other Indo-European dialects shows that the ground stock of words in each of them must have been essentially identical, though however also from this point of view it may be easily proved that the original Indo-European was split up into different dialect-groups. But the parallelism is not confiined merely to the external resemblance of certain vocables, it extends also to the special significance attached to them, as is not very often the case. Words generally considered to be synomymous in reality convey, as often as not, very widely different ideas, for every sound-symbol stands for an infinite number of particular shades of meaning. The meaning of a word can therefore be visualised never by a point but by a circle. It is but rarely that two such circles fully coincide with each other, specially when the words concerned belong the different languages.

But in the case of Indo-European dialects such coincident circles are not altogether rare. The father was conceived of primarily as the protector by the ancient Indo-Europeans. The word *pitā́* (cf. Gr. *patḗr* etc.) is connected with the root *pā-*'to protect' and its formal difference from *pātā́* 'protector' proves but its hoary antiquity. The highest god of the Indo-European pantheon was therefore called *dyaús pitár*, Gr. *Zeũ páter*, Lat. *Jupiter*, etc. The Roman patrician father was in reality the protector not only of his own children but also of his whole clientele. It is this old Indo-European conception of the father which explains that from the the middle ages downwards even monks vowed to celibacy are called father. But the father as the begetter also occupied a high place in the imagination of the original Indo-Europeans, for beside *pitā́* etc. we also find words such as Skt. *janitā́*, Gr. *genetṓr*, Lat. *genetrix* etc.,—all signifying 'father'. Even where different vocables are used, the idea conveyed by them is often identical. It is certain that man was regarded by the ancient Indo-Europeans as the earthly being *par excellence* as opposed to the gods, the celestial beings,—*devá* signifies simply 'celestial'. Thus Lat. *homo*, Goth. *guma*, Lith. *žmũ* is derived from an I.-E. root * *ĝhzem-* signifying 'earth' which has given rise to Skt. *kṣmā́* and Gr. *chthṓn*. An exact semasiological parallel to this group of words may be found in the word *martya* in classical Sanskrit. In the Vedic language however *mártya* as well as *márta* signifies man as a mortal being. That the Indo-Europeans were familiar also with this conception of man as opposed to gods as immortal beings is proved by Gr. *brotós*, Av. *mašya* etc. Similarly the conception of the elements of nature as it obtained among the ancient

Indo-Europeans is fully reflected in Sanskrit and elucidates the analogous conceptions of the ancient Indians. Thus both for fire and water we find in the Indo-European dialects one set of words in neuter and another in masculine or feminine. Thus for 'fire' Skt. *agní* (m.) Lat. *ignis* (m.) Lith. *ugnis* (its fem. gender is of later origin) etc. on the one hand, and Hitt. *paḫḫur*, Gr. *pũr* German *Feuer* (all neuter) etc. on the other. Water too was sometimes regarded as an animate object as is proved by Skt. *ā́paḥ*, Lat. *aqua*, Goth. *aha* (all fem.), and sometimes as inanimate, cf. Skt. *udakám*, Gr. *húdōr*, Goth. *watō* (all neuter). An explanation of this curious phenomenon is to be found in the fact that both fire and water were worshipped as something supernatural and were also used in their daily life by the ancient Indo-Europeans. *Agní* is the designation of the fire-god but Gr. *pũr* signifies only the kitchen fire. In the RV. *ā́paḥ* is always used in connection with moving waters, but *udakám* signifies the still, inanimate water whose only characteristic feature is its capacity to make things wet,—hence its connection with *unátti*. It is curious to note that when this originally neuter stem was applied to moving waters an animate gender was attributed to it, cf. Lat. *unda* 'wave'.

Thus the Indo-European origin of Sanskrit is unmistakable from whichever point of view it may be considered. What is more, Sanskrit is still an Indo-European dialect in all essential features. Unless Sanskrit is studied in this light as part of a vast system of languages a full comprehension of its forms and structure cannot be possible.

VEDA AND AVESTA.

The various branches of the original Indo-European have been enumerated in the previous chapter. Each of them gave rise to numerous independent dialects already in prehistoric times. But all of these branches are not equally autonomous from the view-point of comparative grammar, for almost each of them has special relations either with the original Indo-European or with other Indo-European dialects. It is quite certain that the various Indo-European tribes branched off from the original stock at different times. Some linguists are inclined to believe that the forefathers of the Hittites were the first to branch off from the original stock, or rather that Hittite and the original Indo-European are branches of a still older *Grundsprache*. According to this view Hittite would not be a sister dialect of Sanskrit and Greek but an aunt to them. The other Indo-European dialects known to us may be regarded as sisters of the same parentage, but a few pairs of twins can be clearly distinguished among these sister dialects. Thus the Italic and the Celtic branches represent one pair of such twins, just as the Baltic and Slavic branches represent another. These pairs have not only retained all the essential features of the original Indo-European but each of them is further characterised by a series of special common linguistic innovations. It is these special common linguistic innovations unknown to the original Indo-European which reveal the twinship of particular pairs of Indo-European dialects. The particular pair of twins with which we are concerned in the present chapter is that constituted by the Indic and the Iranian branches of the original Indo-European.

The explanation of common linguistic innovations in two particular Indo-European dialects is quite obvious. We have to assume that the original speakers of these languages used to live together for sometime even after they had detached themselves from the main body of Indo-Europeans, and, what is more, that they used to speak *one* language during that period. Thus it is universally recognised that there was a time when the forefathers of the Iranians and the Vedic Aryans used to live together and speak a common language. That they lived together for a pretty long time and were members of the same society is conclusively proved by the remarkable cultural affinities between these two peoples, which cannot fail to strike everybody who has ever looked into the Veda and the Avesta. The important religious reformation introduced by Zoroaster lent a highly spiritual aspect to the old Iranian religions, but still the substratum of an older culture, almost identical with that of the Veda, is unmistakable in the Avesta, and, what is more, both the Veda and the Avesta seem to breathe the same spirit.

But, if possible, even more striking are the linguistic affinities between the older literatures of India and Iran. It has been often said,—and it is hardly an exaggeration, that the Avestan language stands closer to Vedic than the classical Sanskrit of Kālidāsa. The difference between Avestan and Vedic is in fact not greater than that between some of the Greek dialects known from inscriptions, and the structures of the two languages are so similar that an Avestan sentence can often be translated into Vedic simply by applying to each word the phonetic laws of Vedic. Thus the Avestan passage Y. 10, 8 :

yō yaθā puθrəm taurunəm haoməm vandaetā mašyō
frā ābyō tanubyō haomō visaitē baešazāi

is equivalent to Vedic :

yó yáthā putrám táruṇam sómam vandeta mártyaḥ
prá ābhyas tánū́bhyaḥ sómo viśate bheṣajā́ya.

Here only in the last word do we find a difference of form, in all other cases the difference is merely phonological. A more eloquent proof of the close relationship between the two languages can be hardly imagined. Yet it is not enough to convince the linguists of any special relation existing between Vedic and Avestan. They will argue that the apparent similarity may be simply due to the fact that both these two languages are known from a very early date when they had not yet had enough time to change much from their original Indo-European prototype. In fact so long as the apparent similarity consists merely in the retention of the characteristic features of the *Grundsprache* it cannot prove any special affinity between any two Indo-European dialects. Only a series of common linguistic innovations can prove that, as mentioned above, but there is no dearth of such innovations in Vedic and Avestan.

In the field of phonology the most important common innovation between these two languages is certainly the obliteration of all distinctions between the three original *a*-vowels ĕ, ŏ and ă. In the place of these three distinct vowels in Greek we find only ă in Sanskrit and Iranian, which shows that this far-reaching change in the Indo-European vowel-system had taken place already in the common Indo-Iranian dialect spoken by the common forefathers of the Vedic Aryans and the Iranians. Thus Gr. *epí pétetai*, but Skt. *ápi pátati* and Av. *aipi a-patat*; Gr. *ósse pósis*, but Skt. *akṣí páti* and Av. *aši paitiy-*. Indo-European *ă* of course has remained unchanged in all the three languages, cf. Gr. *ákmōn*, Skt. *áśman* and Av. *asman*. From the extensive use of the vowel *ă* in Indo-Iranian it was thought at first that Sanskrit and Avestan have preserved the old state of things and that this original vowel was split up into *ĕ*, *ŏ* and *ă* in Greek etc. at a comparatively later date. But this view had to be gradually given up, for it was observed that although to all appearance *ă* is a perfectly homogeneous vowel in Indo-Iranian the behaviour of the gutturals preceding it is by no means so simple in these languages. In fact before every *a* for which Greek etc. show an *e*, the Indo-European gutturals assume a palatalised form in Indo-Iranian and in the *Satəm* dialects in general; thus Gr. *te* (<**qᵘe*), Lat. *que* but Skt. and Av. *ca*. Now as this palatalisation is otherwise known in Indo-Iranian only before *i* or *y* (cf. Skt. *ójīyas* but *ugrá* and Av. *draojišta* superlative of *draoga*) it had to be assumed that the Indo-Iranian palatalising *a* must have had an *i*-timbre originally,—in other words, that it was originally an *e*. Once it was thus conclusively proved that Greek has preserved the Indo-European vowel-system more faithfully than Sanskrit by distinguishing between *a* and *e* there was already a strong presumption also in the case of *o* that this vowel too had once enjoyed a separate existence in Indo-Iranian. No direct proof can be brought forward to prove this as in the case of *e*, but here too the *a*-vowels which have to be traced back to Indo-European *o* show peculiar ablaut forms quite unknown to those corresponding to Indo-European *e* or *a*. In certain cases a peculiar alternance between *a* and *ā* is observed in Sanskrit, the shorter vowel appearing before a consonant-group and the longer one appearing before a simple consonant. If in analogous cases *e o* (out of older *ai au* respectively, see above, p. 12) appears before a consonant, its place is taken by *āy āv* before a vowel. Analogy with the alternance *a* : *ā* is quite complete here, for we have to remember that the second element of a diphthong may take up the function of a consonant. Thus, for instance, in the 3. sg. perf. act. *da-dárś-a* but *ja-jā́n-a* (alternance *a* : *ā*), *ci-két-a* but *ji-gā́y-a* (alternance *e* : *āy*), *ju-jóṣ-a* but *su-ṣāv-a* (alternance *o* : *āv*). Now, the corresponding forms in other Indo-European dialects show that in these cases *a* : *ā* is derived from I.-E. *o*; *e*: *āy* from I.-E. *oi* ; and *o* : *āv* from I.-E. *ou* ; cf. Gr. *dé-dork-e, lé-loip-e, eilḗ-louth-e* (from roots *derk-, leip-, leuth-*). The strangely behaving *ă*, which in certain cases shows a short form before a consonant-group and a long form before a simple consonant is therefore derived from I.-E. *o*, as distinct from I.-E. *e* or *a*. This differential behaviour of *a*-vowels derived from I.-E. *o* shows that there was a time when they were still qualitatively different from the other *a*-vowels in the common Indo-Iranian language. It is therefore quite a legitimate and natural assumption that in its earlier stage the Indo-Iranian still retained the old I.-E. vowel *o* which only later changed into *a* and thus coincided with I.-E. *e* and *a*. Yet no *a priori* reason can be shown why particularly the vowels derived from I.-E. *o* should vary in quantity in particular positions. Brugmann attempted to prove that the alternance *a* : *ā* is the normal Indo-Iranian representative of the Indo-

European alternance *e* : *o* in open syllable; cf. Gr. *patéres a-pátores*: Skt. *pitáras tvát-pitāras* ("having you as father"), Gr. *ákmon-a*: Skt. *áśmān-am* Av. *asmān-am*. But Brugmann himself was compelled to give up his theory in view of numerous exceptions, cf., for example, Gr. *gónos*: Skt. *jána*, Gr. *homós* : Skt. *samá*.

We have seen that Indo-Iranian *a* corresponds to I.-E. *e, o, a*. But there is an apparent exception to this rule, and this exception is again a notable common linguistic innovation of Sanskrit and Avestan. Ordinarily Indo-Iranian *ă* corresponds to the I.-E. short vowels *ĕ, ŏ, ă*; but for those *ĕ, ŏ, ă* in Greek, which stand in ablaut relation with *ē, ō, ā* respectively, Sanskrit and Avesta show not *ă* but *i*. To render the picture still more complicated, the homogeneous vowel *ă*, which might be expected in Indo-Iranian, appears in every other Indo-European dialect * and corresponds there to Indo-Iranian *i* and Greek *ĕ, ŏ* or *ă* as the case may be. Thus the short vowel *ĕ* in Gr. *e-té-thēn* (<**e-thé-thēn* through dissimilation of aspirates, see above, p. 10) stands in evident ablaut relation with the long *ē* in Gr. *tí-thē-mi* (original Indo-European root *dhē*). But the weak-grade form of the same root shows an *i* in Sanskrit *hitá* and an *a* in Lat. *fa-c-io*. Similarly the weak-grade form of the Indo-European root *dō-* shows an *ŏ* in Greek (cf. *e-dó-then* as opposed to the full-grade form in *dí-dō-mi*) but again *i* and *ă* in Sanskrit (cf. *á-di-thās*) and Latin (cf. *dă-tus*) respectively. It is still a disputed problem whether this Greek alternance *ĕ* : *ē* and *ŏ* : *ō* is normal and phonetic or

* in the shape of the regular phonetic equivalent of I.-E. *a* in the dialect concerned. Thus in Slavic an *o* corresponds to this Indo-Iranian *i*, for I.-E. *a* had become *o* in Slavic at a very early period.

is based on analogy with the alternance *ă* : *ā* as observed in *stă-sis* : *hi-stā-mi* (Doric) from *st*(*h*)*ā*-, whose weak-grade form shows *i* and *ă* in Sanskrit and Latin respectively (cf. Skt. *sthi-tá*, Lat. *stă-tus*), but most linguists are now inclined to believe that the variety of sounds appearing in Greek has preserved something old and original which has escaped the other languages striving for uniformity in one form or other, —in the form of *i* in Indo-Iranian, and elsewhere in the form of *ă*.

Now it is almost universally accepted that the original I.-E. sound to which an *i* corresponds in Indo-Iranian and an *a* elsewhere (always excepting Greek), was a weak and indeterminate vowel,—in fact a weak-grade ablaut form of either of the three long vowels *ē*, *ō* and *ā*. Short root-vowels generally disappear altogether and short diphthongs forfeit their first components in weak-grade form ; but long vowels always leave something behind in similar cases even though it be a weak and hardly articulate vowel. In the technical terminology of linguistics this weak vowel is called *Schwa Indogermanicum** and is transcribed by an inverted *ə*. Now this *ə* has normally given rise to *i* in Indo-Iranian but coincided with I.-E. *a* in all the other dialects excepting Greek. But if it is accepted that the multiplicity of forms in Greek is not due to later analogical influence of the alternance *ă* : *ā* but an authentic relic of the original Indo-European, it has to be admitted that however feebly this Schwa Ind. might have been pronounced it still succeeded in preserving its

* The word 'schwa' is taken from Hebrew grammatical literature where it designates a similar weak vowel. Sometimes it is also called the neutral vowel. But if the variety of sounds appearing in Greek is not due to mere form-analogy it would be incorrect to call it neutral.

original timbre in each case. Thus the evidence of Greek would seem to suggest that when derived from *ē* the *Schwa Indogermanicum* had an *e*-timbre, when from *ō* an *o*-timbre and when from *ā* and *a*-timbre. The apparent anomaly that sometimes to a Greek *ĕ ŏ ă* an *i* and not the usual *a* corresponds in Indo-Iranian (cf. Skt. *pitá*, O. Pers. *pitā* : Gr. *patḗr*) can therefore be fully explained. For we have seen that the vowel in question was originally none of the three ones for which an *a* may be usually expected in Indo-Iranian, but a sound of quite a different character, so feebly pronounced that its exact vowel-timbre in each case was completely lost in all the languages excepting perhaps in Greek.

The ablaut *ā* : *ə* however naturally appears to be too violent. It seems unlikely that the long vowel *ā* would be reduced to mere *ə* when the accent is shifted. One would be tempted to believe *a priori* that a reduced vowel *ă* has to be postulated as the intermediary step between *ā* and *ə*, so that the whole ablaut series would be *ā* : *ă* : *ə*. In fact in Skt. we do find traces of this short *ă* alternating on the one hand with *ā* and on the other with *ə* (> *i*), cf. *rā-* : *rá-tna* : *arí*. This and a few other similar cases of alternance between *ă* and *ā* have given rise to the belief that the I.-E. *ə* sporadically appears as *a* in Skt. It would be more accurate however to take this *a* as the intermediate reduced step between *ā* and *ə*. Hirt is inclined to believe that such an intermediate reduced step has to be postulated also in the case of ablaut *a* : O (zero). In other words, in his opinion, even a short vowel cannot disappear altogether in the first instance without leaving some trace behind—an intermediary reduced-vowel step has to be postulated also in this case.

Hirt would thus postulate the ablaut series *a* : *x* : O (zero). The existence of such a series cannot be proved by means of examples out of Skt., but certain instances of vowel alternance in Greek suggest that Hirt's series is quite plausible. Thus at the side of the normal grade form *bélos* we have the nil grade form *bl-ē̃nai*. But whence comes the aorist form *bal-eĩn*? Here it is quite clear that the radical vowel was not altogether lost; it is here the carrier of a distinct syllable (*ba-leĩn*). Hirt therefore suggests that here we are confronted with the intermediary reduced vowel between *a* and O (zero).

In the treatment of the semi-vowels *i̯* and *u̯* the languages of the Veda and the Avesta differ from all the other Indo-European dialects in one respect: in the earliest stage of both these languages *i̯* before *i* and *u̯* before *u* seem to have been dropped even though the result was a hiatus. Skt. *śréṣṭha* for instance has its exact counterpart in Av. *sraēšta*. But it is to be noted that in the RV. *śréṣṭha* is often trisyllabic, and analogous forms clearly show that the stem is *śrai̯*. For the relation between *śréṣṭha* and *śrīrá* is precisely the same as that between *śáviṣṭha* and *śūrá* or *dáviṣṭha* and *dūrá*. It is quite clear therefore that the original form of *śréṣṭha* must have been **śrayiṣṭha*. The trisyllabic value of *śréṣṭha* is thus explained. But the Avestan form shows that **śrayiṣṭha* had to pass through the stage **śraïṣṭha* before reaching the final form *śréṣṭha*. In the RV. both the forms *revát* and *rayivát* are current. But Av. *raēvat* shows that the former represents the older form, derived from Indo-Iranian **raïvat* <**rai̯ivat*. In Skt. *rayivát* the *y* was analogically introduced at a later date.

Due to the same phonetic law the verb-forms in Skt. which would normally begin with *yi-* show an initial *i-* in the older language. Thus the desiderative stem of *yaj-* is *iyakṣ-* in the RV. But in the classical language the initial *y* was re-introduced analogically and there the corresponding stem is *yiyakṣ-*. This mode of re-introducing *y* is current already in the Brāhmaṇas, for there the desiderative stem of *yam-* is *yiyaṃs-*, and the corresponding form of *yabh-* is *yiyaps-*. Yet in certain cases the older form persisted also in the classical language, cf. *iyāja* (perfect) from *yaj-*. In all the cases of desiderative mentioned above, the *i* of the reduplication syllable is at least of Indo-Iranian antiquity as we shall see below, but from the extant Avestan texts no form can be quoted which would prove a similar loss of initial *y* before *i*. The sound combination *yi* in medial position is not altogether rare in Skt., cf. *ápāyi* (aor. pass. of *pā-*), *ājáyi* (loc. sg. of *āji*), etc. But all these forms are later analogy-formations.

The similar disappearance of *v* before *u* is not exactly comparable with the phenomenon discussed above, firstly because there is no sure Avestan example which would prove the validity of this law also for old Iranian, though however it is admittedly quite probable, and secondly because in none of those numerous cases of the loss of *v* before *u* in Skt. is the vowel in question of Indo-European origin. In fact the combination *ṷu* was extremely rare in the original Indo-European. In most cases the *u* in Skt. which causes the loss of the preceding *v* is derived from an Indo-European *r*-sonans (I.-E. *ṝ* normally becomes *ūr* in Skt.), cf. Skt. *úrā* 'sheep' : Gr. *varēn* ; Skt. *ūrmi* : O.H.G. *walm*, etc. This is a peculiar feature of Skt. alone, for in analogous cases the original initial *v* is regularly retained in Avestan, cf. Skt. *úras*: Av. *varō*, Skt. *ūrṇā*: Av. *varəna*, etc. In Skt. perfect forms such as *uvā́ca* (: *vac-*), *uvā́sa* (:*vas-*), etc. an initial *v* has been evidently dropped before *u*, but this *u* too is of properly Indian origin, for in all these forms the original reduplication syllable was *va-* and not **vu-* (cf. *vavā́ca*). In analogous cases the reduplication syllable is invariably *va* in Avestan (cf. Av. *vavača*). No parallel to these Skt. perfect forms with initial *u* can therefore be found in Avestan.

Both in Skt. and Avestan an Indo-European *s* undergoes a similar transformation after *i, u, r* and gutturals. It appears that already in pre-Indo-Iranian age the Indo-European *s* in these positions had become an *š*-sound, the exact nature of which cannot be determined. In Skt. this *š*-sound further changed into cerebral *ṣ*. The Indo-European superlative suffix *-isto* appears as *-iṣṭ(h)a* in Skt. and *-išta* in Avestan. The sibilant of this suffix is the same as that in the comparative suffix *-(i)yas* which appears both in Skt. and Avestan. The transformation of the dental *s* into *ṣ* in Skt. and *š* in Avestan is therefore clearly due to its position after *i*. The suffix *-su* in loc. pl. shows a dental *s* after *ă*, but after *i* and *u* it is invariably *-ṣu* in Skt. and *-šu* in Avestan, cf. Skt. *agní-ṣu, aktú-ṣu* and Av. *xšaþri-šu, vaŋhu-šu*. The same change of *s* may be observed in both the dialects also after *r* and *k*, cf. Skt. *tṛ́ṣṇā*, Av. *taršnō*: Goth. *þaursjan*; Skt. *ukṣitá*, Av. *uxšeiti*: Gr. *auxánō*.

This characteristic of Skt. and Avestan is however shared also by the Balto-Slavic languages, for in the original Balto-Slavic too the Indo-European *s* seems to have become an *š*-sound in similar positions. The transformation of *s* into *š* after *i* out of Indo-European *ə* may however be regarded as a peculiar feature of Indo-Iranian alone ; even in the Balto-Slavic languages nothing parallel can be found, for in them, as in all other non-Indo-Iranian dialects (excepting Greek), I.-E. *ə* coincided with I.-E. *a* and therefore did not give rise to an *i* which might have wrought this change. Thus Skt. *kraviṣ* 'flesh', Av. *xrvišyant* 'blood-thirsty', Gr. *kréas* (<I.-E. **qrevəs*). The Greek personal ending *-asthēs* in 2. sg. aor. med. has its exact counterpart in the Skt. *-iṣ*-Aorist ending *-iṣṭhās*. The initial vowel of this ending is *a* in Greek and *i* in Skt.,—which proves that in the original Indo-European it was *ə*. Here we find again that an *i* <I.-E. *ə* has cerebralised a dental *s* in Skt.

In the field of morphology one of the most striking common innovations of Skt. and Avestan consists of the employment of *u* as the reduplication vowel in present and of *i* or *u* as reduplication vowel in perfect, particularly in the case of verbs with a radical *i* or *u*.

It is generally assumed on good grounds that the reduplication vowel was originally always *i* in present and always *e* in perfect, which latter naturally became *a* in Indo-Iranian. Yet however this distinction between present and perfect was not preserved intact in any Indo-European dialect, and the original state of things in this respect was very much disturbed in the Indo-Iranian dialects. But what is of particular interest to us here is to note that the disturbances are exactly the same in Skt. and Avestan. In both these dialects *i* is still predominently the reduplication vowel in present, cf. Skt. *tiṣṭhati* Av. *hištənti* (: Gr. *histēmi*), Skt. *siṣakti* Av. *hišaxti*, Skt. *iyarti* Av. (*uz*)*yarāṭ*, etc. But the influence of the perfect reduplication with *e* on the present reduplication may be clearly perceived already in the Indo-Iranian era ; cf. Skt. *dádāti*, Av. *daδaiti* though the corresponding Greek form *dídōsi* still shows the original *i* in the reduplication syllable. In the same way Skt. *dádhāti* Av. *daδaiti* (: Gr. *títhēsi*), Skt. *jáhati* Av. *zazāhi*, etc.

The opposite influence of present forms on the perfect was however even more far-reaching, so that even the anomalies of present reduplication were transferred to perfect reduplication by analogy. In all this Avestan goes hand in hand with Skt. At first the present-reduplication vowel *i* crept into perfect reduplication in the case of roots containing an *i* ; cf. Skt. *didvéṣa* Av. *didvaēša* (: *dụis-*), Skt. *ásiṣāya* Av. *āhišāya* (: *sāį-*). Gradually however this *i* made its appearance also in the case of some of those roots which contained no *i* ; cf. Skt. *vivásvān* Av. *vivaŋhušō* (: *vas-*). The only other quotable form of this type in Skt. is the doubtful *vivakvā́n* (from *vac-* ?), but several examples may be quoted from Avestan ; cf. Av. *diδāra* beside *daδāra* : Skt. *dădhā́ra*, etc. In the same way the reduplication vowel *u* invaded the perfect forms after it was firmly established in present reduplication. It is quite evident that on the proportional analogy of *diṣṭáḥ*, *diṣáte* : *didiṣṭána* (imperative) a form *jujuṣṭana* with an *u* in the reduplication syllable automatically came into being on the basis of the simpler unreduplicated forms *juṣṭáḥ juṣate*. Gradually in Skt. *u* became the normal reduplication vowel in present in the case of roots containing an *u*, but in Avestan the corresponding forms still often show the original reduplication vowel *i* ; cf. Skt. *jújoṣate* but Av. *zizušte*. But the analogical *u* is found also in Avestan, cf. Skt. *śúśrūṣati* : Av. *susrušəmnō*. From the present this analogical *u* now gradually made its way also into perfect and in Skt. it became even the normal vowel in perfect reduplication in the case of roots containing an *u*, just as in present ; cf. Skt. *ruródha* : Av. *urūraoδa*, Skt. *tūtā́va* : Av. *tūtava*, etc. Only two Skt. roots in *-ū* have retained perfect forms with the original *a* in the reduplication syllable, e.g. *babhū́va* from *bhū-* and *sasū́va* (beside *suṣuvé* !) from *sū-*. Yet Avestan perfect forms of the former prove that in the Indo-Iranian age both *a* and *u* could function as the reduplication vowel of *bhū-*, cf. *bābvarə* (perfect of intensive) and *bvāva* (to be read as *buvāva*).

The peculiar passive aorist in *-i* is another striking common innovation of Skt. and Avestan of which no parallel can be found in any other Indo-European dialect ; cf. Skt. *ávāci* : Av. *avāčī*, Skt. *śrā́vi* (augmentless form in injunctive) : Av. *srāvī*, etc. The origin of this form, which is so common in Vedic that it came to be substituted for the proper third person of any aorist middle that is used in a passive sense, is quite obscure. It is all the more striking therefore that in Avestan (and Old Persian) this isolated passive aorist form appears in exactly the same form and exercises the same syntactical functions.

Though not so obscure, but hardly less striking is the element *u* which characterises the third person sg. and pl. of imperative in active both in Skt. and Avestan. That forms like Skt. *bháratu*, *bhárantu* : Av. *baratu*, *barəntu* are nothing but proper injunctive forms extended by the particle *u* was recognised long ago. It is curious to note in this connection that the deictic particle *u* is very often used after imperative forms in the RV. and often it is an essential part of the form itself ; cf. *éto* (*éta* + *u*), *tápo* (*tápa* + *u*). It is very probable that this deictic particle was permanently joined to the I.-E. injunctive forms in the Indo-Iranian age in two cases of special frequency and gave rise to the Skt. and Avestan imperative forms referred to above, for which parallel forms can be found in no other Indo-European dialect. In two other cases the personal ending of imperative exhibit analogous innovations both in Sanskrit and Avestan. In 2. pers. sg. act. the usual ending is sometimes increased by *-na* in Skt., cf. *kár-ta kár-tana*. A similar phenomenon may be observed only in Avestan, where we find both the forms *bara* and *baranā* side by side. In 1. pers. sg. both the endings *-ā* (subj.) and *-āni* are current in Skt. and Avestan and this is again a remarkable linguistic innovation common to both. The ending *-āni* very probably stands for **āna*, of which the element *-na* is doubtless identical with the *-na* of *kár-tana*. Now it appears that already in the Indo-Iranian age this ending **āna*, clearly of subjunctive origin, had been changed into *-āni* on the analogy of subjunctive forms ending in *-i*. It is curious to note however that the imperative forms in *-tāt*, which are abundant in Skt. and have their origin in the Indo-European age, cannot be traced in Iranian.

In noun inflexion many common linguistic innovations may be observed in Skt. and Avestan. One may conveniently begin with the ending *-nām* in gen. pl. which is so common in these two languages. The I.-E. gen. pl. ending was *-ōm*, both for consonant and vowel stems. But in Skt. although for consonant stems the older ending has been retained on the whole, a new form *-nām* has been substituted for it in the case of all vowel stems, the only exception in this respect being *devā́m* (for *devā́nām*) in the phrase *devā́m* *jánma*. Yet however, it is not altogether a specific Skt. or Indo-Iranian innovation, for it is very probable that the ending *-nōm* used to be applied to feminine *ā*-stems already in the I.-E. epoch, cf. O. H. G. *gebōno*, O. Norse *runono*. Perhaps for *ī* and *ū*-stems too the same old alliance with the ending *-nōm* has to be postulated, for feminine forms such as Lat. *regīna*, Gr. *aischúnē* prove the I.-E. antiquity of their alliance with an (analogical) *n*. But this is all that can be said in support of the pre-Indo-Iranian existence of the ending *-nām*. The *-ānām* of *a*-stems is an Indo-Iranian innovation. It is true that in Avesta the ending *-ānām* is met with only once (*mašyānąm*, Skt. *martyānām*) and in all other cases we find only the ending *-anąm*. But the latter may be easily a defective writing for *-ānąm*, which is rendered all the more probable by the fact that in Old Persian the only form known is *-ānām*. On the analogy of *a*-stems those in *i* and *u* too began to employ *-nām* instead of *-ām*, and that already in the Indo-Iranian period, cf. Skt. *girīṇā́m* : Av. *gairinąm*, Skt. *vásūnām* : Av. *vohunąm*, etc. Yet Skt. is often left in the lurch by Avestan in these cases, for in it *i* and *u*-stems often take the older shorter ending *-ām* in gen. pl., cf. Skt. *sákhīnām* but Av. *hašąm*, Skt. *paśūnā́m* but Av. *pasvąm*. This shows that Skt. has gone farther than Avestan in generalising the ending *-nām*. Skt. forms such as *nṝṇā́m*, *pitṝṇām* (derived from *ṛ*-stems) and further *caturṇā́m*, *gonā́m*, *ṣaṇṇā́m* have no parallel in Iranian.

The declension of feminine *ā*-stems shows again a series of striking common innovations in Skt. and Avestan. The case-suffixes for Instr., Dat., Abl.-Gen., Loc., and Voc. singular of *ā*-stems show peculiar forms in both these languages which cannot be found in any other Indo-European dialect. The old Indo-European ending *-ā* in Instr. sg. is also used for *ā*-stems in Skt. and Avestan, specially in the case of stems in *-yā* and *-tā,* cf. Skt. *sukṛtyā́ avīratā,* Av. (*uštanō.*) *činahya yesnyata.* It is possible however that in both these cases the shorter ending is due to haplology :—*-yā* may stand for *-yaya* and *-ta* for *-tāta* (i.e.*-tāt-ā*). But in both the normal ending is the analogical *-ayā,* which was originally at home in the pronominal declension. The Dat., Gen.-Abl. and Loc. sg. show disyllabic endings in Sanskrit, characterised by the common element *-āy-*: *-āyai,-āyāḥ,-āyām.* The corresponding Avestan endings are *-ayāi,-ayå* and *-ayā̆,* the initial short *a* of all of which may be due either to defective writing or to the analogy of the ending *-ayā* in Instr. sg. In the other Indo-European dialects the corresponding case-suffixes are monosyllabic and such as would correspond to the Indo-Iranian endings if their common element *-āy-* was taken away. It is clear therefore that already in the Indo-Iranian epoch this *-āy-* came to be joined to the *ā*-stems in all these cases. Only a guess can be made as to the origin of this *-āy-*: perhaps it is analogically derived from the *ī/yā*-stems which have the endings *-yai,-yāḥ and -yām* in Dat.,Gen.-Abl. and Loc. sg. ; cf. *devyái, devyā́ḥ, devyā́m.* In the original Indo-European the *ā*-stems came to have the same ending *-āi* both in loc. (*-ā+i*) and dat. (*-ā+ai*). The post-position *ā* was attached to the locative ending in the Indo-Iranian epoch* to distinguish it from the dative ending,—whence Avestan **-āyā.* Further extended by the mobile element *-am,* which plays such an important part in nominal and pronominal declension in Skt., it gave rise to the Skt. ending *-āyām.*

* Or even still earlier, for the *ā*-stems in Lithuanian too seem to have extended the loc. sg. ending by the post-position *e* ; cf. Lith. *-oj-e.*

On the analogy of this *-āyām* on the one hand and the endings *-yai, -yāḥ, -yām* of *ī/yā*-stems on the other, the element *-āy-* was introduced also into the endings of dat. and gen.-abl. of *ā*-stems in Skt. and Avestan (Bartholomae, Wackernagel). Lastly in Voc. sg. the *ā*-stems both in Skt. and Avestan have the ending *-e* (in Avestan beside it also the ending *-a*) which cannot be paralleled by any other Indo-European language; cf. Skt. *sarame*, Av. *raziště* (but also *pouručištā*). The origin of this ending *e* in Voc. sg. is quite obscure, and it is all the more striking therefore that it is common both to Skt. and Avestan. In the other I.-E. languages the Voc. sg. ending of *ā*-stems is usually *-a*, which may be either derived from *ə* or, as the analogy of *i* and *u*-stems suggests, may be simply the shortened form of the *-ā-* of the stem in unstressed position ; cf. Gr. *óphis* : *óphi*, *pēchus* : *pēchu*, *númphē* : *númpha*. In no wise however can this *-a* be connected with the Indo-Iranian ending *-e*.

It is well known that in Skt. the *i*-stems take the ending *-au* in loc. sg. which is evidently taken from the *u* stems. The original I.-E. ending in this case was *-āi* (cf. Goth. *anstei* : loc. *anstai*), and this ending actually seems to be retained in Skt. *Agnāy-ī* which, according to the genial interpretation of Brugmann, signifies nothing but "the female near *Agni*". With the exception of this sole instance in all other cases this original ending was replaced by the analogical ending *-au* not only in Skt. but also in Avestan, for there too the *i*-stems beside the regular ending show the same analogical form in loc. sg., though however the forms in question are used exclusively as infinitives ; cf. *haθra.jatå* 'to kill all of a sudden', *hubərətå* 'to nurse carefully' (the final *-å* of these forms stands for *-au*). On the strength of Greek forms like *pólēi* (trisyllabic) <**pólēvi* (stem *poli-*) it was suggested that this analogical transfer of the case-suffix of loc. sg. is even of I.-E. antiquity, for **pólēvi* was interpreted as **pólēu̯+i*, of which *-ēu̯* corresponds to Indo-Iranian *-au* and *i* is nothing but the original locative post-position attached to the form at a later stage. Yet however these peculiar loc.-forms might have arisen independently on the soil of Greece as Brugmann has pointed out.

Beside the endings *-(i)yā* and *-inā*, the only ones current in classical Skt., the *i*-stems often take the shorter ending *-ī* in the older language; cf. beside *utiyā́, matyā́, dhāsínā* also *ácittī*. This shorter ending in instr. sg. is again without any parallel in the other Indo-European languages if the Avestan is excepted. There, with one sole exception, namely *haša* = Skt. *sákhyā*, the *i*-stems take only this short ending in instr. sg.; cf. *ašī, čisti* etc. Avestan *u*-stems similarly know only the shorter ending *ū* (written *-u*), cf. *mainyu, daēnu, vohu* etc.,—the sole exception in this case being *xraθwā* = Skt. *krátvā* (ending *(u)vā*). It is quite likely therefore that in the earliest Vedic the *u*-stems knew also the shorter ending *-ū* in instr. sg., though however no un-ambiguous form can be quoted form the extant texts to prove its existence.

All these and various other common linguistic innovations conclusively prove that Skt. and Avestan are to be regarded as a pair of twins within the brotherhood of Indo-European languages. Yet we have to bear in mind that neither Skt. nor Avestan represents a homogeneous language,—each of them contains a number of distinct dialects associated with different ages (and regions). It is natural therefore that the earliest Skt. agrees best with the earliest Avestan. It is to be noted, however, that in various respects the oldest Avestan is more archaic than the oldest Skt. In the earliest Avestan Gāθā dialect, for instance, the old thematic personal ending *-ā*(<I.-E. *-ō*) in I. sg. is still retained, but even in the earliest Skt. there is hardly any trace of it. Already in the earliest Vedic the athematic ending *-mi* has been generalised as in later Avestan. The working of Bartholomae's law according to which the group 'sonant asp. + surd' becomes 'sonant + sonant asp.', is again more archaic in the Gāθā dialect than in the earliest Skt., in which both the earlier and later forms are found side by side. It has been pointed out in the previous chapter that I.-E. roots with initial and final aspirates appear with an initial aspiration in Skt. when the final aspiration is dropped, mostly on account of contact with an *s*. But there are not a few exceptions to this rule in older Skt. Thus the aorist stem of *dah-*(< **dhağh-*) is *dakṣ-* (not *dhakṣ-* as to be expected) and the desiderative stem of *duh-* (<**dhuĝh-*) is *dukṣ-* (not *dhukṣ-*). These *d*-forms appeared to be so anomalous to the Vedic commentators that in the Padapāṭha actually *dh*-forms are given for them. The reduplicated stems *baps-* and *jakṣ-* (derived from *bhas-* and *ghas-* respectively) are still more striking, for they have no aspirated form at all at their side. All this shows that the combination 'aspirate + *s*' exercised the same influence on a preceding aspirate as an aspirate alone. In other words, we have to assume that at least in these cases the law of dissimilation had acted at a time when, due to contact with *s*, the final sonant aspirate had not yet become unaspirated tenuis (*k-s*, *t-s*, *p-s*). The obvious other alternative is that the group 'son. asp. + *s*' had given rise to combinations *gzh* (<*gh-s*), *dzh* (<*dh-s*) and *bzh* (<*bh-s*) (metathesis of aspiration according to Bartholomae's law). These sonant groups at once give the impression of being older than the surd ones. The apparent exceptions to the law of dissimilation are therefore nothing but the result of the same law acting at an earlier stage. Every doubt on this score will be set at rest if the Avestan forms are compared. In analogous cases the Gāθā dialect shows only the sonant groups ; cf. *diwžaidyāi* (*-bž-*, written *-wž-*, from *-bh + s-*), *aoγžā*(*-γž-* from *-gh + s-*) etc. In the later Avesta however the surd groups sometimes occur ; cf. *hangərəfšāne* (*-fš-* from *-bh + s-*), *daxša* (*-xš-* from *-gh + s-*). It was pointed out in the preceding chapter that in a very few cases in the RV. a neuter plural takes a singular verb. In this respect too the Gāθā dialect is distinctly more archaic than the Vedic, for this incongruence is the rule in it just as in Greek. In later Avestan however such constructions are rare.

In comparison with later Avestan however Skt. is distinctly more archaic, for later Avestan actually shows some of the characteristics of Middle Iranian dialects. Inter-vocalic consonants tend to become spirantic in it and the dual number is gradually got rid of. Confusion in the use of cases, already well-nigh hopeless in the Gāθās, becomes still more confounded in later Avestan. The various moods and tenses are no longer distinguished between, subjunctive forms are used in indicative, and the prohibitive particle *mā*, which is connected only with the injunctive in the Gāθā dialect just as in Skt., appears also in connection with optative in later Avestan.

In striking contrast to all other Indo-European dialects Avestan, or Iranian as a whole, resembles Skt. in one important respect : the subsequent development of both, although absolutely independent of each other, has been strikingly similar. Phonology, morphology and syntax of Middle Iranian dialects are unmistakably analogous to those of Middle Indian ones. The same general tendencies, which were inherent in the two respective basic languages, found expression in their later descendants in the same or similar ways. This is again a powerful, though indirect, evidence in proof of the close affinity of Skt. to Avestan.

Comparison with Avestan is therefore indispensable to an historical study of Skt. On innumerable points, both regarding general principles and particular details, Avestan throws light on the history of Skt. as the above rapid comparative survey has shown. Who would, for instance, believe that the original form of the familiar Skt. root *brū-* was *mrū-* if the verb *mrav-* was not actually found to occur in the Avesta ?

VEDIC ORTHOEPY.

The earliest monument of the Sanskrit language is the Ṛgveda, the date of which however cannot be fixed with certainty. Yet the language of the Ṛgveda is so much akin to that of the Gāθās of Avesta that they may be considered to belong to approximately the same age, and as the language of the Gāθās is by no means very far removed from that of the Old Persian inscriptions of the sixth century B. C., the Ṛgvedic language may be roughly dated about 1000 B. C.

How many centuries earlier the Aryans had entered India it is impossible to say. The earliest unmistakable proof of extra-Indian connection of the Vedic Aryans is furnished by the Mitanni of northern Mesopotamia. Their capital city *Vaššuǧǧanni* has almost a Sanskrit name (i.e. *Vasujani*). Whether the Mitanni themselves were an Indo-European tribe is still doubtful, though it has been suggested by no less a person than Forrer that they might have been the forefathers of the Medes of Persia. What is however universally accepted is that the ruling class among the Mitanni, who called themselves Maryanni, were actually an Indo-Iranian—perhaps even an Indian—tribe, and that the Vedic gods mentioned in the treaty-records (about 1400 B. C.) of the Mitanni people, e.g., *In-da-ra, U-ru-van-a* etc., were worshipped by these Maryanni rulers. It is however still a disputed point whether these Maryanni-Indians had marched westwards from the border-land of India or were still on their march eastwards to India.

The archaeological discoveries of the last twenty years have thrown a flood of light on the early history of various Indo-European tribes, though their original home still remains unknown. The position of the Hittites is unique in this respect, not only because they are the connecting link between the oldest Indo-Iranians (i. e., the Maryanni) and the oldest Greeks (the *Aḫḫiyāvā*), but also because their language is the earliest known Indo-European dialect. It is however necessary to bear in mind that what is meant by "Hittite" in common parlance is not the language of the Hittite people of Biblical fame. The Hittites who had conquered Anatolia before 2000 B. C. and had their chief centre at *Hattušaš* (modern Boghaz-keui) were a non-Indo-European tribe. The people of *Nešaš* in the same region were on the other hand linguistically Indo-European, and under *Muršiliš* I (about 1800 B. C.) they conquered *Hattušaš*. Hence the name "Hittite" has come to be associated with the language of the non-Hittite conquerors, although its only correct designation would be "*Nešian*."

The discovery of the *Aḫḫijāvā* people is another epoch-making archaeological achievement of recent times. It is usually accepted to-day that they are the forefathers of the Achaeans of Greece, but as to the country where they were settled at the time of their contact with the Hittites expert opinion still vacillates between the western fringe of Asia Minor, the island of Rhodos and the mainland of Greece. This uncertainty is due to the scantiness of material. From the available data it appears that during the reign of the Hittite monarch *Muršiliš* II (1340 B. C.) the king *Antaravaš* (Andreus !) was the ruler in *Aḫḫijāvā* and the island of *Lazpaš* (=Lesbos), and his brother

Tavaglavaš (= Eteokles ?) was by him appointed king of *Mellavanda* (?). In the days of the Hittite king *Hattušiliš* III (1280 B. C.) the *Aḫḫijāvā* king *Attaršijaš* (Atreus !) took possession of the kingdom of a vassal of the Hittites, and fifty years later he attacked the island of Alasia-Cyprus which was apparently under Hittite dominion. In the year 1227 B. C. the Pharao Merneptah mentions the sea-faring *Akaivaš* along with the *Turša, Sakalša, Sardanna* etc. as confederates of the revolted Libyans. It should be noted that among the sea-faring peoples against whom Ramses III fought in Syria (1190 B. C.), instead of the *Akaivaš* are mentioned the *Danona* (= Homeric *Danaoi*) "in their islands." It has been suggested therefore that the *Aḫḫijavā* kingdom of Rhodos (?) had been destroyed by the Danaoi before 1190 B. C.

About the year 1800 B. C. there took place other events of great importance for the history of the early Indo-Europeans. About this time Babylon fell into the hands of the Kassites and Egypt was invaded by the Hyksos. The Kassites need not have sung Ṛgvedic hymns as they marched into Babylon as Brunnhofer actually suggested, but that Aryan elements were actually present in their language is proved by Kassite proper names like *Indabagaš*, and it is significant to note that the sun-god was called by them *Suriyaš*. The Hyksos period of Egyptian history is a complete blank. Yet from the fact that the Hyksos introduced the horse into Egypt it may not be unwarranted to assume that there was an Indo-European sprinkling among them, for the Indo-European culture was the horse-culture *par excellence*. It is significant that one of the oldest literary compositions in an Indo-European dialect is a manual of horse-training. The library of Boghaz-keui has yielded among its many treasures a most interesting work composed by one Kikkuli from Mitanni in the Hittite language which deals exclusively with this subject, and, beside the numerals, some of the technical terms used in it are almost Sanskrit, e. g. *aikavartanna*.

All this multifarious evidence seems to suggest that sometime about 2000 B.C. the various tribes of the Indo-European barbarians ousted from their unknown original home traversed the wide plains of Eurasia in all directions , and a particular branch of them pushed on to India after spending some time in Iran together with the forefathers of the Iranians. They were the forefathers of the Vedic Indians.

The Ṛgvedic Indians seem to have completely forgotten their pre-Indian associations, although they were still predominantly nomadic in their habits of life. The *grāma* continued to signify till a comparatively late period not a settled village but a roving clan of wandering shepherds as is clearly proved by the legend of Śaryāta Mānava recorded in various Brāhmaṇas. Geographically they were still confined to the land of the five rivers. The earliest days of the Vedic Indians had been anything but happy. From the arid regions of Iran and Central Asia they stumbled across the frontier barriers only to be appalled by the fury of a subtropical clime, and they had to make their way into the plains of India only in the face of fierce opposition from the aboriginal inhabitants, whom they never ceased to curse and condemn in their hymns.

Inspite of such an eventful career the Vedic Indians failed to develop a poetry of high order like the Homeric Greeks, for already from the plains of Iran they had brought with them the cult of sacrifices which continued to dominate the intellectual life of the Indians till almost the present day. Originally the sacrifices were meant to placate the gods and to persuade them to confer favours, but soon the sacrifices assumed a mystic importance and the gods themselves sank to the status of mere pretexts for them. Thus they gradually lost all their personal characteristics, and the same endless cycle of phrases, epithets and adjectives came to be applied to almost every one of them irrespective of their original functions and attributes. Ṛgvedic poetry therefore lacks the colour and flavour of the Homeric epics.

Yet, for the history of the languages of the Indo-European world the Ṛgveda is undoubtedly the most important work, for, excepting the Hittite inscriptions it is the oldest known linguistic monument of the Indo-European peoples. But before dealing with the language of the Ṛgveda, it is necessary to try to reconstruct its text as accurately as possible. For although the Indians through all the ages have paid the closest attention to the Ṛgveda it is quite certain that its text had been originally much different from what it is to-day. But it is possible to restore the original text, at least to some extent, by a careful study of the Ṛgvedic metres, and, what is more, the restored text reveals many important linguistic characteristics which it would not have been otherwise possible to discover.

All the parts of the Ṛgveda are not equally old. The so-called family maṇḍalas (II—VII) represent the oldest part of the Ṛgveda whereas the tenth maṇḍala is decidedly the latest. The ninth maṇḍala is linguistically quite heterogenous, for the hymns addressed to Soma have been collected in it from every part of the Ṛgveda. The remaining first and the eighth maṇḍalas are really old, but the hymns of various groups of priests have been collected in them.

The word *pāvaká* may be taken up as a convenient example of how the original text of the Ṛgveda has been later tampered with. Later Indian grammarians were at a loss to know why the feminine of *pāvaka* is *pāvakā* and not *pāvikā* as Pāṇini would have it. According to Pāṇini a word ending in *-aka*, the element *-ka* of which is suffixal, would assume the aspect *-ikā* when the feminine suffix *-ā* is attached to it. For all that we know of Sanskrit grammar the element *-ká* of *pāvaká* is actually suffixal and the vowel that precedes it is also a short *ă* as Pāṇini requires, and yet this short *ă* is not changed into *i*. It is because appearances are altogether deceptive here. In the present text of the Ṛgveda this word is in fact always *written* as *pāvaká*, but the metre shows that it has always to be *read* as *pavāká*. As the vowel preceding the suffix *-ka* is in this case long *ā* and not short *ă* (as the *written* form implies) Pāṇini's above-mentioned rule finds no scope here. This is the obvious explanation of the apparently irregular feminine form *pāvakā* in Sanskrit, and it clearly shows that for an adequate comprehension of the Vedic language, it is always necessary to know how it was actually read, and for this purpose we have to depend mostly on the metre. In the case of *pāvaká* the evidence of metre always points to the reading *pavāká*, cf. RV. III. 17. 1 *śocíṣkeśo ghṛtánirṇik pāvakáḥ*; VI. 1, 8 *prétiṣaṇim iṣáyantam pāvakám* etc.

Pāvaká is one of the few words which have been systematically misrepresented in the present text of the Ṛgveda. Much more important however is the case of certain phonemes of very frequent occurrence which have been similarly misrepresented in it. *Ya* and *va* for instance have very frequently to be read as *iya* and *uva* in the older parts of the Ṛgveda. Besides the evidence of the metre the Vedic literature is full of notices which leave no doubt on this score. The TS. VI. 1, 2, 6 quotes RV. V. 50, 1 in the slightly altered form *víśve devásya netúr mártο vṛṇīta sakhyáṃ, víśve rāyá iṣudhyasi dyumnáṃ vṛṇīta puṣyáse* and comments thereon : *saptákṣaram prathamám padám aṣṭákṣarāṇi tríṇi*. The second pāda thus consists of eight syllables according to the author of the TS. although according to the written text it has no more than seven. It is to be concluded therefore that the word *sakhyám* was actually read as *sakhiám*. The word *svàr* is written as monosyllabic by the Vājasaneyins, but in the Taittirīya texts it is invariably written as *suvár* (dissyllabic). But even the Vājasaneyi texts, when they speak of the number of syllables in *svàr*, invariably give it as two. Cf. ŚB. 2, 1, 4, 14 ; 11, 1, 6, 5 ; 14, 8, 6, 4. This is all the more remarkable, for here we have before us prose texts which could not be influenced by considerations of metre. In the same way the word *rājanyà* is said to consist of four syllables and *dyaús* of two respectively in the Śatapatha Brāhmaṇa (5, 1, 5, 14 ; 14, 8, 15, 1), and when the same Brāhmaṇa (14, 8, 15, 3) further states that the words *prā́ṇopānó vyānáḥ* (in a prose passage) make up altogether eight syllables, we have only to infer from it that the word written as *vyānáḥ* was read as *viyānáḥ*.

But it is not always safe to accept the opinion of the authors of later Brāhmaṇas is this respect, for not infrequently they have overdone their part and dissolved the semi-vowels into their component parts even where such a procedure is neither warranted by the Ṛgvedic metre, nor is supported by the evidence of other Indo-European languages. Thus, excepting once the word *satyá* is always dissyllabic in the RV., and this is perfectly as it should be, for its Gothic counterpart *sunja* (<**sundi̯a*) clearly shows that the semi-vowel *y* is here of Indo-European antiquity. Yet the ŚB. 14, 8, 6, 2 declares it to be tri-syllabic: *tád etát tryákṣaraṃ satyám íti*. Similarly the word *áśva* which occurs very frequently in the RV. is almost always dissyllabic, for here too the semi-vowel *v* is of Indo-European origin, cf. Lat. *equus* (<**equ̯os*), and in the word *tvác* too the metre leaves the semi-vowel undissolved, for on the evidence of Gr. *sakós* (<**tu̯akos*) it is as old as that in *áśva*. The semi-vowel *v* is indissoluble also when initial in suffixes (*-vant*, *-vāṃs* etc.) and in the sound-complex *-nv-* of roots of class V. Similarly *y* is indissoluble in the relative pronoun *ya-*, the gen. sg. ending *-sya*, the comparative suffix *-yas-*, as well as in the present-element *-ya-* and the future-element *-sya-*.

The dissolution of semi-vowels into their original component parts has however to be carried on not only in the stem-forms as shown above, but sometimes also in the endings. It was suggested in the first chapter that the consonantal endings beginning with *bh-* are probably nothing but *bhi* (>Gr. *-phi*) extended by different elements in different places. This theory finds welcome support in the fact that the semi-vowel *y* has actually to be dissolved into *iy metri causa* in these endings, in which case the first element always turns out to be *bhi*. Thus the mantra *ukthaṃ vācīndrāya devebhyaḥ* is said to consist of eleven syllables in AB. 3, 12, which shows that not only the words *vāci indrāya* have to be read with hiatus, but also that the form *devebhyaḥ* accounts for four syllables, which has hence to be read as *devebhiaḥ*. The distinction between strong and weak declensions of *i*- and *u*-stems can be comprehended only when the semi-vowels are dissolved into their component parts (see below), and the very existence of the frequent secondary suffix *-iya* can be discovered almost solely on the basis of readings restored by dissolving ihe semi-vowel *y*.

Reduplication of a final nasal after a short vowel when a vowel follows (Pāṇini 8. 3. 12) is a peculiar law of euphonic combination in Sanskrit, and except in a very few sporadic cases in some early Greek inscriptions nothing of the kind can be pointed out in the other Indo-European languages. It is futile to try to explain away this phenomenon as due to the effect of stress accent, for it is quite certain that in the age of the Ṛgveda the accent was still predominantly musical. A close scrutiny of the cases of this reduplication in the present text of the Ṛgveda clearly shows us however how it came about, and moreover it will help us to improve the text in many places as it lies before us to-day.

It is again with the help of the metre that it is possible to determine where the reduplication of the final nasal is necessary and permissible and where it is due merely to analogy. In fact the metre shows that the reduplication is necessary where after the nasal a final consonant has been dropped*, but where no such final consonant has been dropped the reduplication is not permissible at all, although in the vulgate text of the RV. it is regularly

*Of a group of consonants at the end of a word only the first remains and the rest are dropped in Sanskrit.

reduplicated also in these cases. Thus the final *n* in participal forms such as *śóśucann, āpánn, prathávann, āpṛṇann,* has to be reduplicated on the evidence of the metre, but in the case of endingless locatives such as *mūrdhán, ékasmin,* and vocatives such as *puruhanman, vajrin* the reduplicated nasal actually disturbs the metre, for in the case of the participles the final nasal was followed by a *t* whereas in the locative and vocative forms the nasal itself was final. Cf. e. g.

RV. 6, 66, 2 : *yé agnáyo ná śóśucann idhānáḥ*
RV. 6, 1, 4 : *śravasyávaḥ śráva āpann ámṛktam*
RV. 4, 53, 2 : *vicakṣaṇáḥ prathávann āpṛṇann urú,*

In all these cases of participle present the reduplication of the final *n* is necessary on metrical grounds, and it is certainly no mere accident that the reduplicated nasal here represents an original *nt.* But in the case of vocatives such as *puruhanman, vajrin,* e. g.

RV. 8, 70, 2 : *índraṃ tám śumbha puruhanmann ávase yásya dvitā́ vidhartári,*
RV. 1, 80, 11 : *yád indra vajrinn ójasā,*

and locatives such as *mūrdhán, ékasmin,* e. g.

RV. 6, 45, 31 : *várṣiṣṭhe mūrdhánn asthāt,*
RV. 8, 45, 34 : *mā́ na ékasminn ā́gasi,*

the reduplicated nasal as given in the traditional text of the RV. actually disturbs the metre, for unlike the participles dealt with above, here the nasal had been always final. It is to be concluded therefore that the final redactors of the RV. started reduplicating the final nasal of the participles in reminiscence of the actual pronunciation of the original authors of the hymns, but were soon led astray by mere appearances and began to reduplicate the final nasal also in locatives and vocatives where it had never been followed by another consonant. This confusion had taken place already in the Ṛgvedic period, for sometimes in the text of the RV. even the reduplicated nasal of an endingless locative seems to be metrically justified.

The form *ékasmin* referred to above deserves special mention for several reasons. To its ending *-smin* correspond Avestan *-hmi* (e. g. *kahmi, čahmi*) and Pāli *-mhi* (cf. also Prākrit *taṃsi*<**tásmi*). In other Indo-European languages too there is no sure trace of *-smin*, rather of *-smi*. This naturally raises the suspicion that perhaps the original ending in this case was actually *-smi*, which was later extended by *-n* when endingless forms of *n*-stems in loc. sg. gave rise to the illusion that the *n* itself was an ending. Moreover in a few cases the metre too shows the ending *-smin* to be nothing but *-smi*, cf. RV. I, 174, 4-5 :—*śéṣan nú tá indra sásmin yónau ; váha kútsam indra yásmiñ cākán*. It is quite clear that *sásmin* and *yásmin* here have to be read as if they were without the final *-n*.

Curiously similar to this reduplicated final *-n*, which is sometimes historical and sometimes analogical as shown above, is the euphonic *t* which according to Pāṇini VIII. 3. 30 can be optionally inserted between a final *n* and an initial *s* (e.g. *san saḥ* > *sant saḥ*). But the metre is here of no avail. Here too the *t* is not due merely to a phonetic phenomenon (as in cases like *vatsyāmi*<**vas-syāmi* etc.), but had its origin in those forms in which a *t* had been actually dropped after the final *n*. Afterwards however the reduplication was analogically extended also to those cases where no consonant had been dropped after the *n*. Thus in RV. 10, 40, 12 *á vām agant sumatir vājinīvasū* the euphonic *t* in *agant* is actually of historical origin, but when the same dental appears also after the vocative *rājan* (cf. RV. 1, 91, 4 *rā́jant soma práti havyā́ gṛbhāya*) it is clearly due to mere form-analogy with *agan* etc. We are now in a position also to explain the peculiar Sandhi of *n*+*ś* into *ñ(c)ch* (Pāṇ. VIII. 3, 31). Here too the process began from those cases where the final *n* was originally followed by a *t*, and this *t* combined with the following *ś* gave rise to (*c*)*ch* (as *tacchiva*<*tat*+*śiva*). Thus in RV. 1, 100, 7 *raṇayañ chū́rasātau* the sandhi of *n*+*ś* into *ñ*+*ch* is historical, for here the participle *raṇayan* stands for older **raṇayant*, and the apparent sandhi of *n*+*ś* is in fact that of *nt*+*ś*, which in ordinary course would give rise to *ñ(c)ch*. But cases of sandhi like *vajriñ chnathihi* (1, 63, 5) or *dásyūñ chimyūn* (1, 101, 18) are cases of pure form analogy, for here the final nasal in question had never been followed by a dental.

Two other curiosities of Ṛgvedic sandhi may be briefly discussed here. It is well known that the abhinihita-sandhi was unknown to the original text of the RV., for almost everywhere the metre shows that the initial *a*- lost through it has to be restored. Moreover there are certain unmistakable indications which go to prove that there was a time when even before an initial *a*- a final -*e* or -*o* used to behave in exactly the same way as before other vowels,—in other words, was changed into -*a*(*y*) or -*av* respectively (cf. RV. 8, 72, 5 *stótava ambyàm* < *stótove amb.*, and *gó-agra* <**gáv-agra*).

The unchangeable pragṛhya-vowels raise a much more difficult problem. As such are regarded primarily the vowels -*ī*, -*ū* and -*e* in dual. As an historical explanation of this aversion to sandhi may be offered only in the case of the nominal dual ending *-e,* it has to be assumed that this characteristic has been analogically extended from here to the other cases. The nominal dual ending *-e* is evidently composed of *-a+ī-* (cf. *sádman-ī, bṛhat-ī́* etc.) and not of *-a+i-* as usually *e* is. Now this *-aī-* naturally assumed the aspect *-àiy-* before vowels, and in such position, the final *y* being dropped, it assumed the form *e.* But this *e* was no longer capable of undergoing sandhi, for a *y* has been actually elided after it ! The *-o* in vocative is never pragṛhya in the RV. although in the Padapāṭha it is always followed by the indicatory *iti.* This anomaly is evidently due to the analogy of words like *átho, utó* etc., each of which is a compound of the particle *u* (*átha+u, utá+u* etc.) and therefore could not make sandhi further lest the particle would be altogether lost sight of. Pāṇini I, 1, 16 ff. quoting these rules from the Ṛkprātiśākhya altogether missed the point in them, and his confusion was still more confounded by Patañjali (see I. H. Q., 1934, pp. 666-669).

One of the most remarkable features of the text of the Ṛgveda is its vowels of dissyllabic value, the most frequent case being that of gen. plur. in *-ām.* Thus we find no less than five cases of this dissyllabic ending in four verses of one and the same hymn VIII, 39 :

2. *tanū́ṣu śáṃsam eṣām*
4. *ūrjā́hutir vásūnām*
5. *sá hótā śáśvatīnām*
6. *agnír jātā́ devā́nām agnír veda mártānām.*

On the evidence of the metre the ending *-ām* in each of the five forms *eṣām, vásūnām, śáśvatīnām, devā́nām* and *mártānām* has the prosodical value of two short syllables, so that they will have to be read as *eṣaam, vásūnaam, śáśvatīnaam, devā́naam* and *mártānaam* respectively. In fact in about one-third of its occurrences in the RV. the ending *-ām* in genitive plural has a dissyllabic value and it is certainly no accident that the same ending has the same dissyllabic value frequently also in the Avesta. Its remote echo can be heard in the corresponding ending also of other Indo-European languages : the circumflex accent of Greek *-õn* and Lithuanian *-ũ*, due to contraction of two different vowels, clearly shows that Sanskrit has here preserved intact the Indo-European state of things. The ending *-ām* is in reality in all the cases cited above the result of combination of the final *a* of the stem with the ending *-ām*.

The dissyllabic value of the ending *-ām* had its origin doubtless in *a*-stems, where contraction of two vowels had actually taken place, and from these *a*-stems they were later easily transferred to other vowel and consonant stems. It may be objected that the dissyllabic value of the ending *-ām* cannot be due to the contraction of the stem vowel *-a* with the *ā-* of the ending, for in the case of *a*-stems the ending in question is *-nām* and not *-ām* from the earliest Sanskrit. But here too the reconstructed text of the RV. will help us out of the difficulty, for the ending *-ānām* as given in the vulgate text of the RV. has sometimes to be read as *-ām*, which is doubtless the original form. Thus in the stereotyped phrase, *devā́nāṃ jánma*, the first word has to be read as *devā́ṃ jánma* on the evidence of metre ! This is one of the extreme cases of tampering with the original text of the RV.

The circumflex accent of this ending in Greek and Lithuanian calls for a word of explanation. In a syllable with acute accent the pitch of voice attains the highest point about its middle, during the first half the pitch being ascending, and in the second half descending. But it is characteristic of a syllable with circumflex accent, as may be still observed in Lithuanian, that two such peak-points are reached in course of one and the same syllable which is, naturally, invariably long. In fact syllables with circumflex accent are as a rule the result of the amalgamation of two separate syllables with two separate peak-points. Now, Greek and Lithuanian have retained in their circumflex the original two separate peak-points although the original two separate syllables have in them been moulded into one. In Sanskrit however the development has been quite different; although in later days the original circumflex came to be regarded as a simple long in it, in the age of the RV. it still retained its dissyllabic value as shown above, presumably with two separate peak-points.

Besides the genitive plural ending *-ām* various other forms of Ṛgvedic noun and verb inflexion contain vowels of dissyllabic value, and most of them can be fully explained historically. The ablative singular ending *-āt* of *a*-stems several times appears to be dissyllabic in value, e. g. *parākā́t* in 8, 5, 31 : *ā́ vahethe parākā́t pūrvī́r aśnántāv aśvinā.* The corresponding ending *-ῶς* in Greek with its circumflex accent again shows that the dissyllabic value of the suffix in question goes back to the Indo-European epoch. In the same way the ending *-ās* in nominative plural has to be read as *-aas* in a few cases, e. g., 1, 105, 5 : *amī́ yé devā́ sthána triṣv ā́ rocané diváḥ* : here the metre clearly shows that *devā́* has to be read as *devaa*. Similarly the word *sómāḥ* in 8, 2, 7 *tráya índrasya sómāḥ* has to be read as *sómaaḥ*.

and in 8, 31, 13, *yáthā no mitró aryamā́ váruṇaḥ sánti gopā́ḥ, sugā́ ṛtásya pánthāḥ* the forms *gópāḥ* and *pánthāḥ* have to be read as *gopaáḥ* and *pánthaaḥ* respectively.

In the field of verbal flexion too the restored dissyllabic reading of the long vowel throws welcome light on the history of Sanskrit. According to Pāṇinean grammar contraction of the augment with the initial radical vowel is obligatory, but, again on the evidence of the metre, the state of things must have been quite different in the Ṛgvedic age. Thus in

10, 49, 3 : *ahám kútsam āvam ābhír ūtíbhiḥ,*
10, 108, 5 : *imā́ gā́vaḥ sarame yā́ aícchaḥ*
and 7, 79, 5 : *ví dṛḷhásya dúro ádrer aurṇoḥ*

the respective augmented verb-forms have to be read as *aavam, aícchaḥ* and *aürṇoḥ* respectively, which shows that the contraction of the augment with the initial radical vowel had not yet been fully achieved in the age of the Ṛgveda. In fact the unanimous evidence of Greek and Skt. proves that the augment was by no means an integral part of the verb-form of tenses for which it was obligatory in the later language. It is in origin a preverb which served to indicate that the action in question had taken place in the past. Wherever other concomittant circumstances sufficed to indicate that the action in question had taken place in the past the augment could be, and used to be, omitted. This is the regular usage in the earliest Sanskrit and Homeric Greek.

The subjunctive mode, which has been almost completely eliminated from classical Sanskrit, plays an important part in the verbal flexion obtaining in the RV., and its special mode-stem is formed by adding to the tense-stem an *a* (cf.

as-á-t). But as this *a* often combines with the thematic vowel (cf. ind. *tápati*, subj. *tápāti*) it is often very difficult to distinguish the subjunctive from the corresponding indicative form. Here again the metre sometimes renders help as it often discloses the fact that the contraction of the thematic vowel with the suffixal *a* of the subjunctive mode had not yet been fully achieved in the age of the Ṛgveda. Cf. e. g. :

6, 67, 11 *ánu yád gā́va sphurā́n ṛjipyám,*

10, 50, 5 *áso nú kam ajáro várdhāś ca.*

The subjunctive forms *sphurā́n* and *várdhāḥ* here have to be read as *sphuraán* and *várdhaaḥ* respectively. Sometimes even indicative forms (of roots ending in *-ā*), which had never been extended by the modal suffix *a*, exhibit a long *ā* of dissyllabic value, but they are clearly due to form-analogy with subjunctive forms. Thus a form like *pánti* (from root *pā-*) may be both indicative (*pā + ṇti*) and subjunctive (*pā + a + ṇti*), and in this case the dissyllabic *ā* may be easily analogically transferred from subjunctive to indicative. But the indicative forms like **pāánti* may also be simply due to form-analogy with *adánti* etc. as Wackernagel has ingeniously suggested. Sometimes the long radical vowels of sigmatic aorist forms such as *akṣār* (9, 98, 2) are of dissyllabic value, but no historical explanation may be offered for them, and they must be regarded as cases of mechanical transfer from their original sources.

In the cases dealt with above the lengthening of vowels may be explained by grammatically analysing the forms concerned ; but this is not always the case. In a large number of cases in the RV., and sometimes even in the later Vedic literature, vowels which according to Sanskrit grammar have been always short, are lengthened apparently only because the metre requires it. As a rule, this lengthening is permitted only in the interior of a verse, and that before a single consonant. Exceptions to this rule are mostly apparent or due to analogy. Thus the final vowel in *ádha* has been lengthened in RV. 4, 10, 2 *ádhā hy àgne* apparently before the consonant group *hy*, but the *pāda* in question has to be actually read as *ádhā hí agne* (with hiatus). Again in RV. 1, 25, 9 *śrudhī hávam* the short *i* of *śrudhi* has been lengthened actually at the end of a *pāda*, but this is clearly due to analogy with the frequent cases of *śrudhī hávam* at the beginning of a verse. Cases of lengthening like RV. 8, 17, 1 *píbā imám* or 8, 34, 11 *raṇayā ihá* are on the other hand ambiguous, for *píbā* and *raṇayā* here may also be regarded as subjunctive instead of indicative forms. These ungrammatical lengthenings are to be explained by the Indo-European rhythmic law which usually did not tolerate a succession of short vowels, as Wackernagel has amply demonstrated.

The basic principle underlying the metrical schemes of those Indo-European languages in which the original musical accent has not been replaced by a stress accent (as in Prākrit, Latin, Germanic and Celtic) is a simple alternation of short and long syllables. In a slightly modified form this scheme may take in two consecutive shorts, but a word consisting of three consecutive short syllables may be normally employed in such a metrical scheme only if its final syllable is made long by position, A succession of four short syllables is an impossibility. Ṛgvedic poets therefore were not free to use all the words current in their language, unless, driven to extremities, they were prepared to do some violence to the morphology of the words at their disposal. This they actually did quite often, metrical considerations apparently being more to them than mere grammatical scruples. For instance, the lengthening of the second syllable in the reduplicating aorist form *ájījanat* (from *jan-*) is purely rhythmical, which was resorted to only because the grammatically correct form **ájijanat* (four consecutive shorts) could not fit into any metrical scheme. The same rhythmic law is at least partially responsible for the curious *āmreḍita* compound *divé-dive* instead of **divi-divi*. This rhythmic law, which led to ungrammatical lengthenings, is certainly of Indo-European antiquity, cf. Greek *sophós* but *sophṓteros*, *hierós* but *hierōsúnē*, etc.

Metrical lengthenings due to this Indo-European rhythmic law are an undeniable fact of the Ṛgvedic text. But it is not true that any and every vowel could be lengthened in this way if only the metre required it. Thus the final vowel of the imperative verb-form *ava* (root *av-*) is very frequently protracted in the Ṛgveda, although it is never the case with the homonymous preverb (*áva*). By a careful study of this ungrammatical lengthening it is possible not only to single out the forms which are particularly susceptible to this apparent aberration, but also to determine, at least relatively, the amount of ungrammatical lengthening in the forms concerned. It is however necessary to remember that the common view which would limit a vowel to one mora or two morae (leaving out the *plutas*) is wholly an arbitrary assumption. The prosodical quantity of a vowel may be less than one mora or more than two morae. But with such vowels we are not greatly concerned here. We are concerned here more with the infinite possible quantities of vowels ranging from one mora to two morae. In classical Skt. vowels of such middle length are not recognised; but in the RV., as also in Prākrit, they are very much in evidence. It is in fact the vowels of such middle length which appear to be ungrammatically lengthened in the RV., as has been definitely established by the researches of Benfey, Zubaty, Arnold and Oldenberg. The author of the Padapāṭha did not know what to do with these apparently protractable vowels. He simply substituted for them the shorter forms prevalent in the later language, although, as Arnold has amply demonstrated, even when used as short, these protractable vowels do not behave in the same manner as the unprotractable ones in the metrical schemes of the Ṛgveda.

It has been proved long ago that the well-known rhythmic law "vocalis ante vocalem corripitur", which is an important factor in Greek and Latin prosody, is derived from the original Indo-European. Traces of the action of this law may be discovered also in Sanskrit, but mostly on the basis of readings restored with the help of the metre. Thus the trisyllabic *mā́péḥ* out of *mā́ āpéḥ* is actually to be read as *má āpéḥ*. This ancient rhythmic law may be perceived also in the cases of hiatus and contraction in the RV. Here hiatus takes place by preference before heavy syllables, and specially before initial vowels followed by a group of consonants. This peculiar tendency of the hiatus clearly shows that in these cases it is not due to the exigencies of metre. In fact, analogous conditions prevailing in Greek prove that here too Sanskrit essentially continues the ancient Indo-European tradition. In Greek too contraction takes place by preference before single consonant and the uncontracted form appears before consonant groups. Thus the word *neós* appears in compound in its uncontracted form before the consonant group -*tt*- in *neottós*, but it is contracted into *nou*- in *noumēnía* before a simple consonant.

Apart from these sporadical cases this rhythmic law is of supreme mportance both in case-suffixes and in primary or secondary derivative suffixes, for it largely determines where the semi-vowels *y* and *v* are to be dissolved into *iy* and *uv* respectively. It has been shown above that the case-ending -*bhyas* has often to be read as -*bhias* (dissyllabic) *metri causa*, but in 120 cases it has a monosyllabic value (-*bhyas*). Now it is significant to note that only in 2 out of these 120 cases the vowel preceding the suffix is short, n all others it is long. The very common suffix -*tya* behaves in exactly the same way; after a long vowel it has always to be read as -*tia* and after a short vowel it is regularly -*tya*. Further, due to this rhythmic law, in the inside of a verse, the pronoun *tya*- is monosyllabic after a light syllable no less than 107 times, and dissyllabic (*tiya*-) only 3 times, and after a heavy syllable it is 26 times dissyllabic and only 7 times monosyllabic. The ancient Indo-European rhythmic law which can be thus perceived in the RV. has left clear traces also in other Indo-European languages, for in Gothic nominal flexion too exactly similar phenomena may be observed; thus of Goth. -*ja*-stems those with a heavy base undergo contraction, e.g. *hairdeis* from *hairdja*-, but such contraction is unknown where the base in question is a light one, cf. *harjis* from *harja*-.

In the whole range of Vedic nominal flexion the old forms have nowhere been so much tampered with as in the case of gen. and loc. du. of *i-*, *u-* and *ṛ*-stems. In classical Sanskrit the endings in question are *-yoḥ*, *-voḥ* and *-roḥ* respectively, but in the RV., on metrical considerations, in the overwhelming majority of cases, these endings have to be read as *-iyoḥ*, *-uvoḥ* and *-aroḥ* respectively, —even after a light syllable. In fact monosyllabic *-yoḥ* occurs in the RV. only in the form *yuvatyóḥ*, which is very probably due to analogy with corresponding case-forms of ī-stems of the devī-type (see below) and monosyllabic *-voḥ* does not occur at all in the RV. and appears for the first time in the AV. In the face of such unanimous internal evidence it may not be unjustified to conclude that in this respect too the RV. represents the older state of things, although sure traces of these restored endings cannot be found in any other Indo-European language.

SANSKRIT PHONOLOGY

It has been shown in Chapter II that Sanskrit vowel-system had assumed more or less its present form already in the Indo-Iranian epoch. But a whole series of new consonants was added to it at a subsequent date, which distinguishes Sanskrit from all other Indo-European languages, including the Iranian dialects. It is the cerebral series of Sanskrit, which is not known in any other Indo-European dialect. The cerebral occlusives were therefore originated on Indian soil. In the Ṛgveda they occur only in medial or final position, and their use is limited in the older language. But they became more and more frequent in classical Sanskrit and the Prākrit dialects.

What is the origin of these cerebral sounds ? Often it has been suggested that the rise of the cerebral series is due to Dravidian influence. This is neither impossible nor unlikely. But it is more important to determine which were those original sounds or sound-combinations which gave rise to the cerebrals in Sanskrit, may be under Dravidian influence. It will be seen that sounds of very different nature have coincided in what appears as the cerebral series in Sanskrit.

In the great majority of cases the cerebral sound in Sanskrit is of Prākritic origin. Already in the Ṛgveda in a large number of words the cerebralisation is due to the influence of *r* on a following dental, *e.g.* *-kaṭa* in *vikaṭá*, *utkaṭa* out of *kṛtá*. The same cerebralisation of an original dental is found even where the previous existence of an *r* in the word in question can be determined only with the help of congeneric forms in other Indo-European languages, *e.g.*, Skt. *káṭu* : Lith. *kartùs*. Here only with the help of Lithuanian can we know that the original form of the familiar Sanskrit word *káṭu* was **kartu*, the sound *r* of which, though it disappeared itself, was responsible for the cerebralisation of the following *t*. This *r* again may appear as *l* in the other languages, for, as will be shown below, a Sanskrit *r* is often derived from an Indo-European *l*. Thus Skt. *jaṭhára* is connected with Goth. *kilþei*. On the basis of this and a few other examples Fortunatov propounded his well-known theory that a Sanskrit cerebral normally corresponds to an Indo-European *l*+dental. But even though Scheftelowitz made an attempt to resuscitate it in a modified form, the theory had to be given up in view of numerous exceptions. The cerebral in Skt. *jaṭhára* for instance, it was pointed out, may be due to the influence of an *r* which is still to be found in the allied form *jartu*. In a large number of cases however the cerebral in Sanskrit is not at all derived from an original dental through the influence of an *r* (or *l*) as described above. In fact the cerebral *ṭ* often alternates with an *ś* in Sanskrit, which, as explained in Chapter I, is derived from the Indo-European palatal occlusive *k̂*. Thus from the stems *paś*- and *viś*- we have the forms *paḍ-bhiḥ*, *viḍ-bhyáḥ* etc. characterised by a cerebral, though it is far from the truth that every stem in *-ś* exhibits a cerebral before a *bh*-ending, cf. *-dṛg-bhiḥ*, *dig-bhyáḥ* from *dṛś*- and *diś*- respectively. Here the question arises, which is not at all easy to solve at first sight, whether the *ḍ*-forms are phonologically regular and the *g*-forms analogical disturbances of the normal working of the phonetic law, or *vice versa*. Yet, as Wackernagel argues, the cerebral has to be considered in such forms to be phonologically regular, for otherwise its appearance at the side of the guttural, which was originally at home only before a sibilant (cf. *dik-ṣu* from *diś-*), cannot be explained. We have therefore to conclude that the Indo-European palatal occlusive *k̂* (which has developed into *ś* in Sanskrit) has under certain circumstances developed into a cerebral in Sanskrit. The question now naturally suggests itself if also the other Indo-European palatal occlusives (namely *k̂h**, *ĝ*, *ĝh*) have in the same way given rise to Sanskrit cerebrals. Before answering that question it will however be necessary to investigate what forms these original Indo-European palatal occlusives have themselves assumed in Sanskrit, for unlike *k̂* (>*ś*), they have no specific unequivocal representatives in Sanskrit. At the outset it may be remarked that the sound *ch*, which has been classed with *c* by all ancient phoneticians (the authors of the Prātiśākhyas and the Śikṣās) and grammarians, should in fact be classed with this *ś* (<I.-E. *k̂*). Sanskrit *ch* has nothing to do with *c*. In fact it is to *ś*, what *kh* is to *k*, or *ph* is to *p*, although *ś* and *ch* are two very dissimilar sounds to-day. This is the reason why Sanskrit *ś* so readily changes into *ch* in Sandhi (cf. *pacchás*<*pad-* + *-śas*). In other words, of the original I.-E. palatal series *k̂ k̂h ĝ ĝh*, the first sound has developed into *ś* in Sanskrit, but the second sound (*k̂h*) has developed into *ch* in it.

Then in Sanskrit two distinct series of palatals have to be distinguished. The older palatal series consists of the sounds derived from the I.-E. palatal occlusives *k̂ k̂h ĝ ĝh* (such as *ś ch* and other sounds to be discussed below), and the later

* No sure trace of this sound unaccompanied by *s* can be found in the original Indo-European.

palatal series represented by *c* and other sounds to be discussed below. These latter are derived from sounds which though themselves were no palatals at all (having been labio-velars or velars in the Indo-European epoch), were yet palatalised at a subsequent date by a following palatal vowel. Thus the initial sound in I.-E. **q̯ᵘe* was no palatal at all, but a labio-velar occlusive. This labio-velar was however palatalised by the following palatal vowel *e*. Thus the palatalised labio-velar appears as *c* in Skt. *ca*. It is clear therefore that the palatalised Indo-European labio-velar *q̯ᵘ* appears as *c* in Sanskrit, but the original I.-E. palatal occlusive *k̂* invariably appears as *ś* in Sanskrit even though the vowel following it be no palatal vowel at all. In fact in the other *Satəm* languages too it appears as a sibilant.

It has been said above that *ch* is to *ś* what *kh* is to *k*. But this is not the whole truth, for etymology and various peculiar features of the sandhi of *ch* clearly shows that an *s* was always present in the original I.-E. sound-complex which has developed into *ch* in Sanskrit. Thus to Skt. *chāyá* corresponds Gr. *skia*. The complex nature of *ch* is also revealed by such sandhi-phenomena as *śivacchāyā* <*śiva* + *chāyā* which have been fully recognised and endorsed by all orthodox Indian grammarians.

In fact the form *chāyá* is immediately derived from **cchāyá*, but as a consonant-combination of this nature was not usually tolerated at the beginning of a word the form in question in initial position came to be pronounced as *chāyá*, though in medial position it continued to be pronounced as **cchāyá* (hence Pāṇini's *śivacchāyā*)*. Gradually however

*Similar phenomena may be observed also in other languages. The Greek word *súkos* is connected with Skt. *śváo* and as I.-E. *ḱw* normally develops

the initial form *chāyā́* got the preponderance over the medial form **cchāyā́* and came to be regarded as the only possible orthographic picture of the word. In the Ṛgvedic prosody however *ch* alone can form position, which clearly shows that the authors of the hymns were fully aware of the complex character of the sound in question They went even so far as to substitute the single consonant *ch* for *cch* even in those cases where the latter form would be more justified from the evidence of other languages or otherwise. Thus the redactors of the RV. would write *gáchati* (instead of classical *gacchati*) although the *ch* in this case, as also in most other cases, goes back to the sound-complex *sk̂*(*h*) (cf. Gr. *báskō*). In the same way the *ch* in *pṛcháti* accounts for I.-E. *sk̂*(*h*), cf O. H. G. *forskōn.**

The close relation between *ś* and *ch* may moreover be inferred from the fact that *śś* has normally developed into *cch* in Skt., cf. *ducchúnā*<**duś-śunā* and *kacchapa*<*kaśśapa* <*kaśyápa.* This shows that in the oldest period of Sanskrit, *ś* had not yet developed into a spirantic sibilant as it is usually considered to be, but was still very much like an occlusive and was hardly distinguishable from the palatal occlusive *c*. It is very likely that in some Vedic dialects at least the cerebral *ṣ* too came to be pronounced like *kh*, for sometimes *ṣ* and *kh* alternate in one and the same word ; cf. the proper name *emuṣa* which occurs also in the form *emukha.* It should be remembered here that the pure sibilant has developed into a

into *ss* in Greek, the form expected is **ssákos.* This form is actually found in the compound *pheréssakos* although *sákos* alone is always pronounced with a single initial *s*..

* It should be noted in this connection that in *Kāṭhaka* orthography *-śch-* is regularly used for the usual *-cch-*(=*ch* in Ṛgvedic orthography.)

kh-like sound also in Old Church Slavic under circumstances similar to those which have cerebralised an *s* in Skt.

The perplexing sound-complex *-kṣ-* may be briefly discussed in this connection. Sometimes a sonant in Avestan corresponds to *-kṣ-* in Sanskrit, *e.g.* Skt. *vákṣat* (*vah-*): Avestan *važut*. In these cases *-kṣ-* is derived from Indo-Iranian *-gžh-* <**ĝhs-* (metathesis of aspiration). In the case of the root *dah-* (<Indo-Iranian **dhaĝh-*) the form *dakṣi* instead of **dhakṣi* suggests that the basic form in question was **dagẓhi* <**dhagẓhi* (see Chapter II). According to Pischel, to this *-kṣ-* in Sanskrit corresponds *-jjh-* in Prākrit. When Skt. *-kṣ-* is derived from *-šṣ-* (<Indo-European *-k̂s-*) its corresponding sound in Avestan is simply *š*, thus Lat. *mox*, Skt. *makṣu*, but Avestan *mošu*. But to Skt. *-kṣ-* <I.-E. *qʷs* corresponds *-xš-* in Avestan, cf. Skt. *vakṣyā́-mi* Av. *vaxšyā*. Yet before a dental, Avestan shows only an *š* also in these cases, cf. Gr. *téktōn*, Skt. *takṣá*, Av. *tašā*. In this and a few other words the Skt. and Greek forms can be reconciled on the assumption of a sound *þ* intermediate between *t* and *s*. Thus Gr. *ktísis* and Skt. *kṣiti* are traced back to I.-E. **kþiti*.

We have seen that Skt. *ś* and *ch* account for *k̂* and (*s*)*k̂h* of the I.-E. palatal series (*k̂*, *k̂h*, *ĝ*, *ĝh*,). But what sounds have the remaining two members (*ĝ*, *ĝh*) of this series developed into in Skt.? It is tempting to assume *prima facie* that I.-E. *ĝ ĝh* have developed into Skt. *j* (*j*)*h*, just as I.-E. *gʷ gʷh* have developed into Skt. *g* (*g*)*h*. But this is only partially true, for not every Skt. *j* (*j*)*h* can be traced back to I.-E. *ĝ ĝh*. In fact each of the two sounds *j* and (*j*)*h* in Skt. may be of two different origins. Thus Skt. *j* may be either derived from I.-E. palatal occlusive *ĝ*, or it may be the palatalised form of the I.-E. labio-velar *gᵘ*, and similarly Skt. *(j)h* may be either derived from I.-E. palatal occlusive *ĝh*, or it may be the palatalised form of the I.-E. labio-velar *gᵘh*. It is therefore of the first importance for the history of Sanskrit to know where *j (j)h* are derived from I.-E. palatal occlusives *ĝ ĝh*, and where they are the palatalised forms of I.-E. labio-velars *gᵘ gᵘh*. In the first case Skt. *j (j)h* are said to belong to the older palatal series, and in the second they are said to belong to the younger palatal series. It is hardly necessary to repeat that *ś* and *ch* (<I.-E. *k̂* and *sk̂h*) always belong to the older palatal series, and *c* (the palatalised Skt. form of I.-E. *qᵘ*) always belongs to the younger palatal series.

It is primarily with the help of the other *Satəm* languages that it is possible to determine where Skt. *j (j)h* belong to the older palatal series. We have seen that of the I.-E. palatal series *k̂ k̂h ĝ ĝh** only the first has developed into a sibilant (*ś*) in Skt. while the others have developed into occlusives in it. But in some *Satəm* languages also the other members of this series (along with *k̂*) have developed into sibilants. Thus if it is found that in a *Satəm* language a sibilant (sonant in this case) corresponds to *j (j)h* of Skt., it may be readily concluded that the Skt. *j (j)h* in question belong to the older palatal series. Thus in *ajá* (cf. Lith. *ožỹs*), *ajína* (cf. O. Ch. Sl. *azĭno*), *vā́ja* (cf. Av. *vāza*), *rajatá* (cf. Av. *erəzata*), *bhūrja* (cf. Lith. *béržas*) etc. the sound *j* in each case belongs to the older palatal series, for the corresponding

* As in most of the *Satəm* languages other than Skt. med. asp. has become media, it is not possible to determine with their help where the original palatal sonant occlusive in question was aspirated. That has to be decided solely from the internal evidence of Skt.

sound in the allied *Satəm* forms is always a sibilant. The *j* of the younger palatal series (*i. e.* the palatalised Skt. form *j* of I.-E. *gᵘ̯*) on the other hand always corresponds to an occlusive and not to a sibilant in the allied *Satəm* forms, cf. *jáni* (: Av. *jə̄ni*), *jīv-* (: Av. *jīvya*), etc.

Internal evidence too is not wanting which helps us to distinguish the older palatal series from the younger in Skt. It is quite clear that the I.-E. palatal occlusive *k̂* (> *ś* in Skt.) has often cerebralised a following dental. It is not unnatural to conclude from this fact that other I.-E. palatals too, namely *ĝ* and *ĝh* ((*s*)*k̂h* has been discussed already), could favour the development of cerebrals out of dentals in Skt. under similar circumstances. This is in fact the truth, though such a transformation is hard to explain phonetically, cf. *váṣṭi* <*váś-ti*, *mṛṣṭá* <*mṛj-ta*, *rā́ṣṭra* <*rā́j-tra* etc.

In short we may assume that those Skt. *j* and (*j*)*h** which, when combined with dentals, gave rise to cerebrals, are to be connected with the older palatal series (*i.e.* are to be derived from I.-E. *ĝ*, *ĝh*), and those Skt. *j* and (*j*)*h* which do not do so are to be connected with the younger palatal series. Thus the forms *á-yāṭ* (<*-yāj-t*) and *á-vāṭ* (<*-vāh-t*) in 3. sg. aor. from the roots *yaj-* and *vah-* respectively, clearly show that the *j* of *yaj-* is derived from I.-E. *ĝ*, and the *h* of *vah-* is derived from I.-E. *ĝh*. This is further corroborated by the evidence of other *Satəm* languages in which the corresponding root-forms exhibit not occlusives but sonant sibilants, cf. Av. *yazaiti* and O. Ch. Sl. *vezą*.

---

* For reasons yet unknown I.-E. sonant aspirate of the palatal series is represented only by *h* and not by *jh* as might be expected. The sound *jh* is altogether a later development in Skt.

Another cause of cerebralisation of original dentals is further to be found in the mysterious influence exercised by the I.-E. sound *z*, which has been completely eliminated from Skt. (along with *ž* and *ẓ*), but has invariably cerebralised a following dental whenever the preceding vowel was not *ă*. In fact there is nothing to wonder at in this phenomenon, for after a vowel other than *ă* the I.-E. *z* became *ẓ*, just as its surd form *s* becomes *ṣ* under similar circumstances. And just as this *ṣ* is capable of cerebralising a following dental, even so the sonant *ẓ* cerebralises a following dental. The only difference lies in the fact that the cerebral sonant *ẓ* itself disappears after extending the preceding vowel in compensation, whereas the cerebral surd *ṣ* remains as before. Thus the word **durdabha* appears as *dūḷábha* in the Ṛgvedic dialect, one of the peculiarities of which is to substitute *ḷ* for *ḍ* in intervocalic position. In fact *dūḷábha* represents **dūḍabha*, which is derived from * *duẓ-dabha* <**duṣ-dabha*. The same process may be observed in the root *īḍ-*, derived from *ij-*(<*yaj-*)*-d*, in the word *nīḍá* (<**ni-ẓḍ-a* <**ni-zd-a* <**ni-sd-a*, in which the element *-sd-* is the weak-grade form of the root *sad-* (<I. E. **sed-*). Similarly *ástoḍhvam* <*a-stoẓ-dhvam* <*a-stoṣ-dhvam* (root *stuṣ-*), where the element *ẓ* has completely disappeared after cerebralising the *dh* of the ending. Here even the compensatory lengthening of the preceding vowel is not in evidence, for the stem-vowel *o* is long by nature.

As a result of the disappearance of the sonant *z* (or *ž*, *ẓ*) not only the quantity of the preceding vowel has changed (been lengthened) as shown above, but it has often also changed its quality. In fact the vowel *a* sometimes becomes *e* and sometimes *o* before a sonant sibilant which has disappeared. Thus *ṣaṣ-daśa*> *ṣaẓ-daśa*>*ṣoḍaśá*, and I.-E. *ma(n)z-dhē*> Av. *mazdā* : Skt. *medhā́*. The apparently irregular form *édhi* (2. sg. Imp.) from *as-* is thus explained. In fact **as+dhi* became **az+dhi*, which naturally gave rise to *édhi*. Thus the transformation of *az* into *e* is a peculiar feature of Skt. which distinguishes it from all other Indo-European dialects including Iranian, and has been responsible for a particular system of verbal flexion which is quite unknown elsewhere. The perfect stem of a root, the radical vowel of which is *a*, often, instead of the required perfect-reduplication, changes that *a* into *e*. Thus from the root *pat-* we have in 3. sg. *pa-pā́t-a* as might be expected from the evidence of other Indo-European languages. But in 3. du. we meet with the strange form *pet-a-túḥ*, in which not only there is no trace of the usual perfect reduplication but in which even the radical vowel *a* has been changed into *e*. In order to explain this and similar forms we have to take recourse to the phonetic law discussed above, according to which *az* becomes *e* in Skt. We will have to imagine that these forms had their origin in roots in which the vowel *e* was the normal result of usual perfect reduplication. This had been indeed the case in roots like *sad-*. In its case the perfect stem *sa-sd-* had naturally become *sa-zd-* >*sed-*. Thus *sa-sā́d-a* : *sed-a-túḥ* (<*sa-sd-a-túḥ*) would be phonetically regular forms. In analogy with *sasā́da* : *sedatúḥ* were later formed *papā́ta* : *petatúḥ* etc.

Next to the cerebrals the most important phonological peculiarity of the Ṛgvedic language is to be found in its treatment of I.-E. *r* and *l*. The behaviour of I.-E. *r* and *l* in fact shows that already in the Ṛgvedic age various dialect groups had been formed, and that the Ṛgvedic language is based on a mixture of the dialects of these groups. It has been pointed out in chapter II that every I.-E. *l* had become *r* in Avestan, and in the RV. too *l* is a rarity. It is fair to assume therefore that in the Indo-Iranian period there was a region where the I.-E. sound *l* had been completely replaced by *r*. The dialect of this region is responsible for those *r* in Skt. to which an *l* corresponds in I.-E., *e.g.* Skt. *rakṣ-* : Gr. *aléxō*; *ric-* : Lat. *linquo* ; *gárbha* : Gr. *delphós* etc. At its side there must have been another dialect in which the I.-E. *l* remained unchanged, cf. *loká*: Lat. *lucus*, *ślóka*: Gr. *klúō* etc. There is however a third group of words in Skt. in which an I.-E. *r* had been changed into *l*, cf. *klóśa* (besides *krośaná* etc.): Lith. *kraukti* ; *lump-* : Lat. *rumpo*, etc. It is no wonder that such a state of things would give rise to considerable confusion in the use of *r* and *l* in the language. Indeed these two sounds alternate not only in the roots and stems as shown above but also in suffixes, cf. *śuk-lá* beside *śuk-rá*, *bhalla* <**bhad-la* : *bhad-ra*. Pāṇini went even so far as to declare at the beginning of his grammar in the *pratyāhāra* sūtras that *ra* in the whole of his grammar signifies not only *r* but also *l*. Later Indian grammarians have followed in the foot-steps of Pāṇini and declared that there is no difference between *r* and *l* (*ralayor abhedaḥ*) in Skt.

These sounds *r* and *l* are important members of the group of semi-vowels (liquids), which are much more complex in character than either vowels or consonants, and the history of the Indo-European vowel-system is so closely interwoven with these semi-vowels through the phenomenon of ablaut that it is impossible to treat of the two groups separately.

A semi-vowel is, as the designation suggests, both a vowel and a consonant, though not at one and the same time. The chief characteristic of a vowel is that it can be the carrier of a syllable by virtue of its durability, whereas a consonant is a momentary sound with no duration at all. It is this possibility of continued duration which distinguishes the vowels from the consonants. *L* alone can form a syllable which *k* cannot. The sound *l* in *table* can be continued to any length without the help of a vowel, which shows that it is itself acting here as a vowel, for it is here obviously the carrier of the second syllable in *ta-ble*. On the other hand in the syllable *la* the function of *l* need not, though it may, be different from that of *k* in *ka*. A dual character can therefore be justly attributed to *l*. The same capacity for duration is inherent also in *m* and *n*, which are therefore likewise included in the category of semi-vowels. The position of *r* however is somewhat anomalous, for a long *r*, which cannot but be trilled, is not a continuous sound. Yet this is merely a technical objection, and for all practical purposes *r* may be regarded as a sound analogous to *l*, *m*, *n*. This double character is not however equally obvious in the case of the other two semi-vowels *y* and *v*, which are, if possible, even more important for the language; but in ablaut-relations they behave in exactly the same way as the other four (*r*, *l*, *m*, *n*).

It is essential to understand at this stage what ablaut is. By ablaut is meant those organic relations among the vowels and diphthongs of congeneric forms which (organic relations) may be inferred to have been present already in the original Indo-European. The vowel-changes concerned, due primarily, if not wholly, to the varying quality and place of accent, may be either qualitative or quantitative. Ablaut may be therefore either qualitative or quantitative. Of these two the quantitative ablaut is by far the more important, though it will not be improper here to briefly discuss at first the simpler qualitative ablaut.

The qualitative ablaut is in the last analysis nothing but the organic interchange between the two Indo-European normal vowels *e* and *o*. Both of them appear in stressed radical syllables (cf. Gr. *phérō* : *phóros*, Lat. *tego* : *toga*). No satisfactory explanation of this interchange between *e* and *o* in stressed syllables has yet been found ; yet it may be safely assumed that the musical quality of the Indo-European accent is primarily responsible for it. As Indo-European *e* and *o* have coincided in *a* in Sanskrit the qualitative ablaut has no special significance for this language. We may therefore concentrate upon the quantitative ablaut, which is much more important not only for Sanskrit, but also for the other Indo-European languages.

It has been stated above that *e* and *o* were the normal vowels in the original Indo-European. It is however possible to qualify the statement further and say that the normal vowel was primarily *e* alone which, due to the peculiar musical quality of Indo-European accent, might sometimes appear as *o*. The third normal vowel of the original Indo-European was *a*, which cannot be brought into organic relation with *e*/*o*. But this *a* was much less frequent than *e*/*o*.

That *e*/*o* should be the normal vowel is almost a physiological truism, for they can be pronounced with the minimum expenditure of energy. In fact, the organs of articulation remain neutral in their pronunciation and hardly a muscle has to be moved. But some amount of tension of the organs of articulation is necessary in pronouncing *a*, while a great deal more energy is expended in pronouncing the extreme vowels *i*, *u*. In all languages not characterised by a sharp expiratory stress accent the extreme vowels *i*, *u* have actually changed towards the normal vowels *e*, *o* in historical times. In case of the opposite movement (*e*, *o*>*i*, *u*) as in Paiśācī Prākrit, it is almost certain that the accent was predominantly expiratory. Thus *e* being the normal vowel, the normal diphthongs would be *e* plus one of the semi-vowels (called co-efficient) *y*, *v*, *r*, *l*, *m*, *n*,—that is to say, *ei̯*, *eu̯*, *er*, *el*, *em*, *en* (or *oi̯*, *ou̯*, *or*, *ol*, *om*, *on*, when the normal vowel is *o*). The extreme vowels *i*, *u* etc., at least in the radical syllables, are always derived from these normal diphthongs, and as such they are always the secondary product of Indo-European ablaut. (It may be mentioned in passing that diphthongs like *iu̯* or *ui̯*, of which both members are extreme vowels, are never of Indo-European origin).

The last sentence requires some amplification, for this is in a nutshell the whole secret of the Indo-European vowel-system. If the above statement is true, every radical *i* is certainly *organically* related to some *i*-diphthong (*i.e.* *ĕi̯*, *ŏi̯* or *ăi̯*) and every radical *u* is certainly *organically* related to some *u*-diphthong (*i.e.* *ĕu̯*, *ŏu̯* or *ău̯*). Instances are not wanting to show that this is really so, though however it may not be possible to point out in each and every case a normal-grade form to a radical extreme vowel, and *vice versa*. We are now in a position to understand that ancient Sanskrit grammarians, like the antique grammarians of Europe, were certainly wrong in postulating the extreme vowels *i*, *u* etc. as the normal ones and the guṇa-vowels *e*, *o* (<*eį*, *eų*) as secondarily derived from them. We will now have to admit on the contrary that the guṇa-vowels are the normal ones, from which are derived the extreme vowels *i*, *u*, etc. on the one hand, and the vṛddhi-vowels *ai*, *au* (<**ēį*, *ēų*) on the other.

The organic relation between *eį* and *i* or *eų* and *u* can be best illustrated by comparing the flexions of *eį*-roots or *eų*-roots with those of the root *as*- (<**es*-).

Let us consider the following flexions of the Sanskrit roots *as*-, *i*- and *uṣ*- :

ás-ti	*s-táḥ*
é-ti	*i-táḥ*
óṣ-ati	*uṣ-ṭá*

It needs but to look at these forms to be convinced that *as* : *s* = *e* : *i* and *o* : *u*. The root *as*- became *s*- through the loss of initial *a* on account of the shifting of accent, but through what loss did *e* in *éti* became *i* in *itáḥ*? The truth is that the Sanskrit *e*, consisting of Indo-European *e*+*i* (: *eį*), has here lost its first component, with the result that its co-efficient *į* has attained the status of an independent vowel *i* in the form *i-táḥ*. In the same way *oṣ*- (<**eųs*-) in *óṣ-a-ti* has become *uṣ*- in *uṣṭá* through the loss of the initial vowel in the original root. We are now in a position also to understand the enigmatic liquids *ṛ* and *ḷ* : they are but the weak-grade forms of the normal-grade diphthongs *er*, *el* (alternating with *or*, *ol*). Thus from the root *ker*- we have *kṛ-tá* and from *kelp*- is derived *kḷp-tá*.

The vowels *i*, *u*, *ṛ*, *ḷ* have thus been explained in the cadre of the Indo-European ablaut system,—we have seen that they are but the weak-grade forms of the diphthongs *ei̯*, *eu̯*, *er* and *el* respectively. But the number of possible diphthongs is not exhausted therewith,—we have still to consider *em*, *en*. On the analogy of *er*, *el*, the weak-grade vowels originating out of *em*, *en* would be *m̥*, *n̥* as they are actually represented in linguistic works. But the real problem for us is to know what are the sounds corresponding to *m̥ n̥* in Sanskrit and other Indo-European languages. It is surprising to note that the phonemes corresponding to *m̥ n̥* normally show no trace of a nasal not only in Sanskrit but also in Avestan and Greek, though in the other Indo-European languages there is a trace of the nasal in their case. Indo-European *n̥ m̥* have in fact normally developed into *a* in Sanskrit, Avestan and Greek. Nothing is easier than to prove this, though it took the linguists many decades to perceive this fundamental fact of Indo-European phonology. The oft-quoted I.-E. form *k̂m̥tóm*> Skt. *śatám* proves the development of *m̥* into *a* in Skt., and the numerous ablaut forms such as *man-* : *ma-táḥ* (<*mn̥-táḥ*) *han-* : *ha-táḥ* (<*hn̥-táḥ*) conclusively prove the same change also for *n̥*. In a very large number of cases the vowel *a* in Skt. is derived from Indo-European *m̥* or *n̥*.

It is necessary to consider at this point another possible source of the Indo-European short vowels. They are primarily derived from *ei̯*, *eu̯*, *er*, *el*, *em*, *en* ; but they may be obviously also the result of the weakening of *i̯e*, *u̯e*, *re*, *le*, *me* or *ne* (samprasāraṇa). That it is more than a mere probability is proved by such forms as *yaj-* : *iṣ-ṭá*, *vas-* : *uṣ-ṭá*. In these cases Skt. *ya*, *va* (<I.-E. *i̯e*, *u̯e*) have been actually weakened into *i* and *u* respectively after losing their vowel co-efficient as the result of the shifting of accent. Similarly

from the root *trap-* we have the nominal derivative *tṛp-rá* (*ra* : *ṛ*). The prohibitive *a* is obviously the weak-grade form of *ne*, thus *ne*> *n̥*> *a*, but there is no sure trace of a Skt. *a* <*m̥* <*me* unless Skt. *a-gāra* is actually etymologically connected with Gr. *mé-garon*.

Sanskrit short vowels may thus be explained in the light of Indo-European ablaut-system, but there remains still to explain the long vowels in the same way,—which is much more difficult to do. Many details of this branch of Sanskrit phonology have not yet been satisfactorily explained.

It may be said on the whole that the long vowels *ī*, *ū*, *ṝ*, *ḹ*, *m̥̄*, *n̥̄* are in the same way directly derived from Indo-European *ei̯ə*, *eu̯ə*, *erə*, *elə*, *emə* and *enə* as the short vowels *i*, *u* are derived from Indo-European *ei̯*, *eu̯*. Such a statement, though true essentially, is hardly satisfactory, for it is clear that sound-groups like *ei̯ə*, *erə*, *enə* cannot be original. Even if it is found that they are the immediate source of the long vowels, we shall have still to enquire from what source are they themselves derived. That *ei̯ə*, *eu̯ə* have actually resulted in *ī*, *ū* in Skt. need not however be seriously doubted, for the examples are sufficiently compelling. Compare e. g.

śayi-tvā : *-śī-ma* (*ei̯ə* : *ī*)

pavi-tra : *pū-tá* (*eu̯ə* : *ū*)

It is not *a priori* evident that *erə* (*elə*) would in the same way give rise to *ṝ* (*ḹ*), but analogous examples leave us no other choice but to accept this equation too. It has to be remembered in this connection however that Indo-European *ṝ* is usually represented by *īr* or *ūr* (after labials) but never by *ṝ* in Skt. Compare e.g.

párī-man (<*pari-man*) : *pūr-ṇá* (*erə* : *ūr*)

śárī-ra (<*śári-ra* ?) : *śīr-ṇáḥ* (*erə* : *ī̆r*)
tarī-ṣyati : *tīr-ṇá* (*erə* : *īr*).

Like *m̥ n̥*, the corresponding long sonants (*m̥̄ n̥̄*) normally appear without any trace of a nasal in Skt., namely as *ā*. An *ā* alternating with *ani* (<I.-E.**enə*) is therefore derived from Indo-European *n̥̄* and is analogous to *ī* alternating with *ayi* or *ū* alternating with *avi*. Such *ā* : *ani* alternance is not rare in the language, though however it will be difficult to point out a sure case of *ā* : *ami* alternance. Compare e. g.

khani-tra : *khā-tá* (*ani* : *ā*=*enə* : *n̥̄*)
jani-tā : *jā-tá* (*ani* : *ā*=*enə* : *n̥̄*)

A nasal was however introduced into these weak-grade forms at a very early date : cf. e.g., *śān-tá*, *śā́n-ti* (from *śami-*) for **śā-tá*, **śā́-ti*. In the post-Ṛgvedic language this unetymological nasal came to be more and more retained in the weak-grade forms.

It is now clear that Sanskrit long vowels *ī*, *ū*, *r̥̄*, *l̥̄*, (*m̥̄*, *n̥̄*) may be satisfactorily explained within the frame-work of Indo-European ablaut-system if we start with the assumption that in the original Indo-European, beside roots of the type *ei̯*, *eu̯*, there were others of the type *ei̯ə*, *eu̯ə* etc. That the roots of the type *ei̯*, *eu̯* were primary has been shown above. Can the same may be said also of roots of the type *ei̯ə*, *eu̯ə* ? In other words, can we trace in the original Indo-European any roots whose normal aspect was *ei̯ə*, *eu̯ə* ? This question has to be decidedly answered in the negative. For it has been shown in Chapter II that the neutral vowel *ə* is nothing but the weak-grade form of the Indo-European long vowel *ē*, *ā* or *ō*. Roots of the type *ei̯ə*, *eu̯ə*, *erə*, *elə*, *emə*, *enə* therefore presuppose roots of the type *ei̯ā, eu̯ā, erā, elā, emā, enā.* In order to explain the long vowels we have thus to assume the existence of ***dissyllabic roots*** as was perceived for the first time by Ferdinand de Saussure in modern times. The ancient Indian grammarians went a great way towards discovering this fact of fundamental importance, but they stopped short at postulating roots of the type *ei̯ə erə enə* as the original ones readily recognisable by the increment *i* (<ə),—the seṭ-roots. It was not possible for them to go further, for it was not known in those days that an *i* might be derived from *ā* through the intermediary stage of *ə*. (More about these dissyllabic roots in the chapter on Verb). The origin of long radical vowels in Skt. should therefore have been as in the following table :—

ei̯ā > *ei̯ə*> *ī*

eu̯ā > *eu̯ə*> *ū*

erā > *erə*> *r̥̄*

elā > *elə*> *l̥̄*

emā > *emə*> *ā* (<*m̥̄*)

enā > *enə*> *ā* (<*n̥̄*)

All this however would remain mere theory unless convincing examples could be found to prove the phonetic changes implied in these equations. But such examples are not lacking. Let us consider the root *ĝei̯ā-*. It is a fundamental law with these dissyllabic roots that in the quotable forms only one syllable may appear in full grade, when the other must show a weak-grade form. The root *ĝei̯ā-* therefore may actually appear either as *ĝi̯ā*, or as *ĝei̯i-* (<*ĝei̯ə-*) which latter may further assume the aspect *ĝei̯-* sometimes, for *ə* phonologically disappears in many positions. The weakest-grade form would of course be *ĝī-* as shown in the above table. Thus if we find in Sanskrit and other Indo-European languages congeneric forms which have to be traced back to *ĝi̯ā-, ĝei̯ə-* : *ĝei̯, ĝī-* we may safely assume that they are ultimately derived from the dissyllabic root **ĝei̯ā-*. Now such forms are actually available. Compare.

jyā-	<**ĝi̯ā-*	
jayi-tā	<**ĝei̯ə-*	
jay-á	<**ĝei̯ə-á*	
jī-tá	<**ĝī-tó*	<**ĝei̯ə-tó*
*ji-tá**	<*ĝi-tá*	<**ĝei̯-tó*

Similarly the forms **śray-iṣṭha* (that is the phonetic value of the written form *śréṣṭha*), *śrī-rá* (<**k̑rei̯ə-ró*) reveal the possibility of the existence of a dissyllabic root **k̑rei̯ā-* in the original Indo-European, and *śáv-iṣṭha* (<*k̑éu̯ə-isto*): *śū-rá* (<**k̑eu̯ə-ró*) presuppose a similar root **k̑eu̯ā-*, just as *dáviṣṭha* (<**déu̯ə-isto*): *dū-rá* (<**deu̯ə-ró*) presuppose **deu̯ā-*. An excellent example of a dissyllabic *elā*-root is afforded by the congeneric forms ***párī-man*** (<**pélə-men, i* in *pari-* has been rhythmically lengthened), *á-prā-t* (<**e-plēt*), *pūr-ṇá* (<**pl̥̄-nó* <**pelə-nó*). An equally convincing example of an *enā*-root is *ĝenā-*, cf. ***jani-tá*** (<*ĝenə-*), *ján-aḥ* (<**ĝen-os* <**ĝenə-os*), and ***jā-tá*** (<**jn̥̄-tó*).

These and numerous other examples conclusively prove that dissyllabic roots actually played a very important part in the Indo-European vowel-system. The long vowels of Sanskrit are organically related to them in the same manner as the short vowels are to the monosyllabic roots, and it is also undoubtedly true that the *seṭ*-roots of the ancient Indian

* The form ***ji-tá*** was possible only when ***jay-*** abstracted out of ***jay-á*** etc. gained the status of an independent root.

grammarians are in fact nothing but these dissyllabic roots (invariably ending in a long vowel) in a disguised form. Yet, nothing can be farther from the truth than to say that all the *seṭ*-roots of the ancient Indian grammarians are derived from Indo-European dissyllabic roots. The tendency of the Sanskrit language has been to progressively extend the sphere of this *seṭ*-vowel, particularly in the field of nominal derivatives and verbal abstracta.

Finally, a few rules about Indo-European roots may be noted which are based on observation :

1. An Indo-European root can begin *and* end with sonant aspirates, but not with pure sonants ! thus **bheu̯dh-* is possible but not **beu̯d-*.

2. A root which begins with an aspirated sonant occlusive cannot end with a surd : Thus **bheu̯d-* is possible but not **bheu̯t-*.

3. A root can never contain two consecutive sonants which may function as consonants. Roots like **teu̯l-*, **tei̯rp-* **moi̯n-* are therefore impossible.

SANSKRIT WORD-FORMATION

Much has been said in the previous chapters about roots, which are usually regarded as the primary ingredients of all languages. But we have seen that if anything can claim to be this primary ingredient, it is rather the *stem*, which, when athematic, may appear to be what is usually called "root". Yet the word "root" has had such a long currency in linguistic literature that every attempt to eliminate it is bound to be attended with considerable difficulty, and provided it is borne in mind that they are by no means everywhere the "primary ingredient" there need be no reasonable objection to using it. Indeed, not only in the verbal system, but also in connection with the various other types of words current in Sanskrit and other Indo-European languages, it is extremely expedient to posit a stock number of "roots" representing the liaison-elements of particular groups of congeneric forms.

These liaison-elements, or roots, were considered to be always verbal by ancient Indian grammarians. This is however wrong, for even within Sanskrit we have clear examples of non-verbal roots, cf. *pad-* (=foot), *mah-* (=great). Indeed it is quite certain that these roots are derived from that period of the original Indo-European, when clear and distinct grammatical categories, such as nouns, verbs, adjectives etc., had not yet been developed. This is proved most strikingly by a patent fact of all Indo-European languages, the importance of which is so easily overlooked seemingly because it is so familiar,—by the fact that all categories of words (verbs, nouns, adjectives etc.) may be derived from one and the same root. There is *a priori* no reason why such vast conglomerates of forms and meanings should be regarded as resting on a few *verbal* roots only. Rather we should consider these roots to have been originally endowed with unspecified undifferentiated meanings, susceptible of closer characterisation as verbs, nouns etc. Formantically, they were naturally nothing but athematic stems. Starting from these bare roots, which may be as often nominal as verbal, we shall briefly discuss in the following the various ways of constituting word-forms, firstly by means of *primary* (*kṛt*) suffixes added to roots, and secondly by means of secondary (*taddhita*) suffixes added to stems formed with primary suffixes. Lastly, we will have to consider the compounds consisting of combinations of different word-forms, in which, again, the lead given by the ancient Indian grammarians is still being followed by modern linguists. Next to the discovery of dissyllabic roots, the classification of compounds is the chief achievement of ancient Indian grammarians.

Of all stems the simplest are naturally the athematic ones with no suffix,—in other words, the radical stems. They are very numerous, and their representatives are to be found among all categories of words, not only in Sanskrit but also in all other Indo-European languages. Thus *dyaú-ḥ* (heaven), *kṣā́-ḥ* (earth), *gaú-ḥ* (cattle), *brū́-ḥ* (eye-brow) are all typical examples of suffix-less radical nouns in Sanskrit. All four are of Indo-European origin, cf. Greek *Zeús, chthṓn, boũs, ophrũs.* The two significant forms, *e. g. rāj-* (nom. sg. *rā́ṭ*) and *viś-*, disclose the prevalence of radical nouns also in other important aspects of life, and *mṛd-* and *vār-*, meaning earth and water, are two other radical nouns of supreme importance. Radical nouns may be formed also of reduplicated roots, of *juhū́* from *hū-*, *dadhṛ́k* from *dṛh-*. Whether simple or reduplicated, the radical stems ending in *-i*, *-u* or *-ṛ* are invariably characterised by the "root-increment" *-t* as was already observed by Pāṇini, cf. *mí-t*, *stú-t*, *kṛ́-t*, as well as *di-dyú-t* from *dyu-*. The origin of this "root-incerement" is not clear. According to Brugmann (Griech. Gr. §212, 1) it is an ablaut-form of the suffix *-to*. But this does not explain why this suffix appears only after vowel-stems in Skt. It has consequently to be separated from the suffix *-t-* in Greek which appears both after vowel and consonant stems.

Next should be considered the stems characterised by the thematic vowel *-a*. Strictly speaking, this thematic *-a* is no suffix at all, for, as shown above, the thematic stems have as good a claim to be regarded as primary ingredients as the athematic ones—the "roots". Yet, from purely formantic considerations at least, it is not only convenient but also more logical to make a separate category out of them, for athematic root-stems may be often proved to have gradually become thematic in course of time, while athematisation of original thematic stems is practically unknown excepting in sporadical cases. The general tendency of all Indo-European languages has been distinctly towards thematising originally athematic stems. Needless to say, the athematic stems are in the first instance related to athematic verbal roots, just as thematic stems are to the thematic ones; but the overstepping of these boundaries is not at all rare or exceptional.

The suffix *-a*, as well as the following suffixes, are to be considered in close connection with the place of accent, for according as the stem is stressed or the suffix, two very different groups of words are originated. It is a general fundamental law of all nominal suffixes, but particularly applicable to the case of this suffix, that forms with accented suffix are generally active in meaning, whereas those with accent on the radical vowel are mostly passive,—and this from the original Indo-European. The active meaning, through a slight dislocation, which is easily understandable, often becomes adjective,—"doer" becomes "doing" (*i.e.* "active"). As a result of this attendant semasiological dislocation the original agent-noun (with the accented suffix) generally appears as adjective in Sanskrit, the original action-noun (with accented radical vowel) appearing at its side as the corresponding nominal form. Thus *śoká* "brilliant" : *śóka* "brilliance" (from root *śuc-*), *vár-a* "choice" : *var-á* "chooser" (= "suitor"), etc. Exactly the same state of things may be observed also in Greek, cf. *tómo-s* "cut" ; *tomó-s* "cutter, cutting," etc. It is clear from the evidence of Greek that this suffix *-a* (I.-E. *-o*) had a predilection for the vocalism *-o* in the root. But it was not always simply so, for examples are not wanting in which the radical vowel appears in an extended grade ; thus in Skt. we have beside *bhár-a*, also *bhār-á*. Similarly in Greek too we find beside *sorós* also *sōrós*. Sometimes, beside the form with a long radical vowel none with a normal-grade one can be traced, cf. Skt. *āmáḥ* : Gr. *ōmós*. But even where the radical vowel appears only in an extended grade the contrast in meaning between the two forms is by no means blurred or obscured, cf. *kā́m-a* "desire" : *kām-á* "desiring" (from *kam-*) ; *śā́k-a* "help" :

śāk-á "helpful". Yet many roots take this suffix in their weak-grade form, cf. *śuc-á, kṛś-á* etc. They are very probably of later origin, and the analogous Greek forms too are to be similarly judged, *zugó-n, lúko-s.*

Already in the Indo-European epoch the suffix *-o* (> *-a* in Skt.) began to be used also after reduplicated stems, cf. Skt. *ca-krá* : Gr. *kú-klos.* But Skt. went much farther than the other languages in associating this suffix with reduplicated stems, cf. *vavr-á* from *vṛ-*, *dadhṛṣ-á* from *dhṛṣ-* etc. But usually it is the intensive stem which is used for this purpose, cf. *vevij-á* from *vij, rorud-á* from *rud-* etc., as well as *carā-car-á, mari-mṛś-á, sari-sṛp-á* etc.

The suffix *-as* seems to be but an extended form of the suffiix *-a* discussed above, for the fields of application of both are equally wide, and the same law of accent determining the meaning holds good also for this suffix, cf. *áp-as* "work" : *ap-ás* "active", *tar-ás* "quick" : *tár-as* "quickness", *máh-as* "greatness" : *mah-ás* "great", etc. This suffix was very productive also in Greek, cf. *nábhas* : Gr. *néphos, śrávas* : Gr. *klé(v)os* etc. The Greek forms prove that *e*-vocalism of the root was normal with this suffix. Yet the roots often appear in a weak-grade form before this suffix, cf. *júv-as* (beside *jáv-as*), *mṛ́dh-as* etc., and sometimes in an extended grade, cf. *vā́s-as, vā́h-as* etc. The abstract nouns formed with this suffix are neuter already from the Indo-European epoch. Yet in a number of cases in Skt. abstract nouns in *-as* assume an animate gender. It is a significant fact about these anomalous forms that the place of accent too in most of them is not on the root as to be expected, but on the ending (MacDonell § 126, 2a), which suggests that these are very probably original adjectives later substantivised.

Thus *rakṣ-ás* (masc.) and *uṣ-ás* (fem.) are to be explained in this way.

The primary suffix *-i* has been very productive in Skt., though in the other Indo-European languages it is not nearly so. Its Indo-European origin is however placed beyond question by such comparisons as *van-í* : O. H. G. *win-i*. It may be identical with the *-i* of heteroclitic *-i* : *-an* stems discussed in next chapter (cf. *ásth-i* : *asth-an*, *ákṣ-i* : *akṣ-an* etc.) and which is clearly in evidence in *vā́r-i*, *hā́rd-i* out of older *vā́r*, *hṛ́d*. The root, when not reduplicated, may appear in all its gradations before this suffix, cf. *kṛṣ-í rúc-i* (reduced grade), *rópi śoc-i* (normal grade), *grā́h-i dhrā́j-i* (extended grade). In the case of reduplicated roots the radical syllable always appears in a weak form, cf. *cá-kr-i*, *já-ghr-i* etc.

The suffix *-is* stands in much the same relation to *-i* as *-as* to *-a*, and that the same function was discharged by the two pairs is proved by the fact that it sometimes actually alternates with *-as*, cf. *máh-is* for *máh-as*. As typical formations with this suffix may be mentioned *jyót-is*, *roc-ís*, *śoc-is* etc. The suffix in *krav-is* however is different, for, as its Greek counterpart *kré(v)as* shows, this *i* goes back to Indo-European *ə*, which was not the original form of the suffix in *van-i* etc. as shown above.

The primary suffix *-u* was extensively used already in the original Indo-European, cf. *svād-ú* : Gr. *hēd-ús*, *pṛth-ú* : Gr. *plat-ús* etc. But its boundaries were greatly extended in Sanskrit so that we find in this language a very large number of formations with this suffix. The two forms quoted above (*svād-ú*, *pṛth-ú*) show that stems both in extended and reduced grades were capable of combination with this suffix, but the form *ket-ú* : Goth. *haid-us* shows that the normal grade too was not excluded from the field in the original Indo-European. In most cases the forms in question are adjectives, and the accent too is accordingly almost invariably on the suffix, *ur-ú, mṛd-ú, tan-ú* etc. The accent on the radical syllable in *céru* (adj.) suggests therefore that perhaps the suffix element here is *-ru*. A primary suffix *-us* is not wanting at the side of this *-u*, cf. *van-ús, vid-ús*. In quite a number of substantives, both masculine and neuter, formed with this suffix, the accent is on the radical syllable, cf. *tápus pár-us* (neuter), *mán-us náh-us* (masc.). This fact makes it doubtful whether the suffix *-us* is ultimately connected with the suffix *-u*, which almost always bears the accent on itself as shown above.

A group of primary suffixes characterised by the common element *-an* (<I.-E.-*en*) had played an important part in the formation of words in Sanskrit as well as other Indo-European languages. The bare suffix *-an* has not been very productive in Sanskrit, but its Indo-European origin cannot be contested in the face of such comparisons as *tákṣ-an* : Gr. *tékt-ōn, ukṣ-án* : Goth. *auhs-in* etc. Of the greatest importance was this suffix for the Germanic languages in which the weak *n*-declension (cf. mod. German *Fürst* : *Fürsten, Fels* : *Felsen* etc.) is nothing but an offshoot of this ancient Indo-European nominal suffix *-en*, which somehow found its way even into the noun-inflexion of these languages. The *n*-flexion of Latin stems too (cf. *Cato* : *Catonis*) is to be explained in this way.

Much more important for Skt. is the suffix *-man* (<I.-E. *-men*), of which the weak form *-ma* (<*mṇ*) too has been an important primary suffix already from the Indo-European epoch, cf. *hó-ma* : Gr. *cheũ-ma* etc. (Brugmann-Thumb,

§ 190). Alternation between *-man* and *-ma* is found also within Sanskrit, cf. *dhár-man* (RV.) : *dhár-ma* (Saṃhitā). The suffix *-man* forms a very large number of derivatives, most of which are neuters accented on the root, but a good many are accented on the suffix and their gender is masculine. The difference in meaning parallel to difference in accent is quite striking in a few pairs of words, thus *brah-mán* (masc.) "priest" : *bráh-man* (neut.) "worship" ; *dhar-mán* (masc.) "ordainer" : *dhár-man* (neut.) "ordinance" etc. The root, as will be seen from the above examples, usually appears in the normal grade ; yet reduced-grade (*bhū-mán, vid-mán*) and extended-grade (*bhā́r-man, svā́d-man*) forms too are not wanting. Quite a number of dissyllabic roots take this suffix, *e.g. ján-i-man, vár-i-man* etc.

The suffix *-van* is doubtless one of the oldest primary suffixes of the Indo-European languages, for different ablaut-forms of it may be observed in the function of independent suffixes from the earliest period, and augmented by the element *-t*, perhaps through the analogical influence of the suffix *-ent* : *-ont* discussed below, it gave rise to the very productive (secondary) suffix *-vant* in Skt., to which corresponds *-vent* in Greek (Brugmann-Thumb § 215). This suffix *-ven-(t)* alternates visibly with the suffix *-ves/-vos*, cf. Hom. *tē̃os*<**tā-vos* : Skt. *tā́-vant*. This alternation of *-n* and *-s* shows that the original suffix in question was *-ve/-vo*, which was extended sometimes by an *-n* and sometimes by an *-s*. The weak-grade form *-un* of this *-ven /-von* attained the status of an independent suffix already at a very early period, cf. *Vár-uṇ-a* as opposed to Gr. **ovor-van-os* (>*Ouranós*) and Hittite *u-ru-van-a*. The normal-grade form of Skt. *mith-un-á* is to be found in Avestan *miθ-van* and within Sanskrit itself we find *śak-un-á* at the side of *śák-van*. But even in the weak-grade form *-un*, this suffix could not forget its close relation to the *s*-forms, for *van*-stems often alternate with *us*-stems in Skt., cf. *pár-van* : *pár-us*, *dhán-van* : *dhán-us*.

Already in the original Indo-European the suffix *-ent* : *-ont* was the only one used to form active participles of the present. In Skt. it has resulted in *-ant* which is only too well-known as the suffix for present and future participles. As in the case of the suffix discussed above (*-van* : *-un*), the weak-grade form *-at* (<*-n̥t*) of this formantic element also attained the status of an independent suffix not only in Skt. but in Greek too (see Brugmann-Thumb § 214). This is clearly perceived in those forms in which this weak-grade suffix is accented, *e.g. vāgh-át* (masc.), *srav-át* (fem.). The stems *s-ánt-* and *d-ánt-*, derived from *as-* and *ad-* respectively, show in a striking manner that the root assumed a weak form before the suffix, as is proved also by the accent which is hardly ever on the root.

The suffix used for the formation of perfect participles (active) is *-vāṃs*. Its weak-grade forms *-vas-* (cf. *vid-vát-su* <*vid-vás-su*) and *-us-* (cf. *vid-úṣ-ā*) are without any trace of the nasal,—which shows that the nasal in *-vāṃs* is inorganic. This is further corroborated by the fact that in Greek too the corresponding suffix is without any trace of a nasal, cf. *tasthi-vás* : Gr. *este(v)ṓs*, *vid-vás* : Gr. *(v)eid(v)ṓs* (Brugm.-Th. §231). This nasal is equally prominent by its absence in the corresponding suffixes in Iranian (Barth., Vorgesch. §209.6). The best way to explain this inorganic nasal in *-vāṃs* is perhaps to assume an analogical influence of the corresponding present participal suffix *-ant*.

The suffixes *-ta* and *-ti* are so similar in function and morphological behaviour that it is impossible not to recognise a close inter-relation between them. On the basis of such Greek forms as *ágnōto-s* : *agnṓs* (<**agnṓts*), *próblēto-s* : *problḗs* (<**problḗts*), Brugmann (Greich. Gr. § 212) ingeniously suggested that this *-to* is nothing but a reinforced form of an original suffix *-t-* which is in evidence in Skt. *kṣi-t, -śru-t, -kṛ-t* etc. (see p. 102). If this is true, we have here an explanation also of the suffixes *-ti -tu*, for they too then may be regarded as formans originated out of this primary *-t-*.

In Skt. the suffix *-ta* is thought of almost solely as the suffix *par excellence* for the formation of past participles. This was doubtless one of its functions already in the original Indo-European, but it was neither its only nor its most important function. Indeed, in languages other than Skt. the number of past participles formed with this suffix, so familiar to students of Sanskrit, is not at all very imposing excepting in Latin. It was in fact originally a nominal suffix comporting active meaning, with the accent accordingly almost invariably on the suffix ; but by imperceptible degrees, this active meaning (*e. g.* "doer") became neutral (*e. g.* "doing") and finally passive (*e. g.* "done"). All these three stages may still be clearly distinguished in Skt. cf. *sū-tá* "charioteer" (active), *dyū-tá* "gambling" (neutral), *ha-tá* "hurt" (passive). The shifting of meaning from active to neutral was sometimes accompanied by a corresponding shifting of accent, *e. g. vā́-ta* "wind", *már-ta* "mortal". Gradually however this suffix came to be more and more identified with the last passive meaning and we actually find passive past participles formed with this suffix almost from every root in Skt. But its rule could never be quite absolute, for from the earliest Indo-European it found a formidable rival in the suffix *-no* discharging identical functions. Like *-ta* the suffix *-na* too gradually became identified with passive participles in Skt., the difference between them being that the latter is never separated from the root by the *iṭ*-vowel which is often the case with *-ta*. The original function of this suffix is best shown by such forms as *svápna* (cf. Lat. *som-nus* but Gr. *húp-nos* with a different vocalism), *dā́-na* (cf. Lat. *dō-num*), of which the nominal accent too is to be noted. But that the participial sense too had been developed already in the parent language is proved by *pūr-ṇá* : Lith. *pil-na-s*. In some cases the language made adroit use of the twin-suffixes by attributing a nominal meaning to the one and an adjective meaning to the other; thus *svápna* (noun) : *sup-tá* (adj.) or *pūr-tá* (noun) : *pūr-ṇá* (adj.).

The suffix *-ti* is almost as productive in Sanskrit as *-to*, and it is hardly less popular in Greek (where it appears as *-si*). It is all the more strange therefore that it is hardly in evidence in Latin,—precisely the language in which the Indo-European suffix *-to* has been most extensively used. Given the sameness of meaning, this suggests *a priori* that the suffixes *-to* and *-ti* were interchangeable to a certain extent at least. All the other details do but confirm this view. In the majority of cases the accent is on the suffix as in the case of *-ta*. Even where the accent is on the root its weak form sometimes shows that the accent had been shifted secondarily: *gá-ti* (from *gam-*), *íṣ-ṭi* (from *yaj-*) are to be explained in this way. The cause of this shifting of accent is not difficult to guess,—it was doubtless of a piece with the usual change of meaning towards nominalisation. That almost all the stems formed with this suffix are of an animate gender (mostly feminine) shows that this suffix too, like *-ta*, formed originally agent nouns and comported an active meaning. In many cases it almost appears to be the feminine counter-part of the suffix *-ta*, cf. *jā-tá*: *ja-tí*, *ma-tá* : *ma-tí*. All this goes to support the view expressed above that *-ta* and *-ti* were originally different aspects of the original suffix (or root-increment) *-t-*.

Though strongly resembling *-ta* and *-ti* both in form and function, the suffix *-tu* can only with difficulty be connected with them, for the root in its case mostly appears in a strong-grade form, cf. *tán-tu*, *mán-tu*, *vás-tu*, etc. Even where the suffix is accented the root sometimes shows a strong form, cf. *jan-tú*. Its Indo-European origin is at any rate guaranteed by Skt. *pi-tú* : Gr. *pí-tu*, Lat. *gus-tu-s* : Goth. *kus-tu-s* etc. This suffix has been largely requisitioned in Skt. to form infinitives. Not only the suffix itself, but also variously strengthened forms of it are used for this purpose, *e. g. -tum*, *-tave*, *-tavai*.

Perhaps the best known active primary suffix in Skt. is *-tar*, which is of Indo-European origin and has been productive in all the principal dialects. Words of such common currency as *pi-tá̄*, *mā-tá̄*, *duhi-tá̄* were formed with this suffix already in the original Indo-European. The forms in question are mostly accented on the suffix when the active meaning is predominant and apparent as the above examples show. But in many cases the basic roots retained their independence in spite of association with this suffix to such a degree that the resultant meaning could not but be participial, in which case, as to be expected, the root was accented. Thus we actually find stems with this suffix directly governing an object like a transitive verb, *e.g.* *dā́-ta vásū* instead of later *dātā́ vásūnām*—"giving riches" became later "giver of riches." The difference in accent between the two forms is significant and instructive.

The thematised form *-t(e)ro-* of this suffix became an independent suffix designating instruments of action already in the Indo-European epoch. Sometimes *-tar* and *-tra* appear after the same root,—*kár-tra* (neut.) : *kar-tā́*, *mán-tra* (masc.) : *man-tā́* etc. Most of the stems in *-tra* are neuter as the accent on the radical syllable would also imply. But there are forms with anomalous accent such as *ne-trá* (neut.). On the whole the suffix *-tra* seems to have been requisitioned to furnish the neuter counter-part of the active suffix *-tar*, and such neuter counter-parts could have been only the instruments of action as distinguished from the agents of action designated by *-tar*.—As a continuous untrilled *r* automatically becomes *l*, it is no wonder to find at its side a suffix *-tlo-* in the original Indo-European. By a curious phonetic dislocation which is still to be explained, this *-tlo-* appears as *-klo-* in Latin and Lithuanian. Skt. *-tra* is therefore often met by *-klo-* in these languages, *e.g.* *pā́tram* : Lat. *pōculum* (<**pōklom*), *arítram* : Lith. *árkla-s*.

Skipping over many other primary suffixes the comparative and superlative suffixes *-īyas* and *-iṣṭha* may be at last taken up for consideration, which offer many interesting features. These two suffixes cannot fail to remind one of the analogous Greek suffixes *-i̯os* (still traceable in *elā́ssō* <**elā́ti̯os-a*, etc.) and *-isto*, the element *-is-* of the latter being nothing but the weak-grade form of the comparative suffix *-i̯os* (*-yas* in Skt.), which is clearly in evidence in Lat. *mel-ior*, *pejor* (<*ped-i̯or*) etc. It is curious to note that no less than four different ablaut-forms of this suffix are used in the Indo-European languages to express comparison. The weakest grade *-is* may be perceived in Lat. *mag-is* (cf. *mag-nus*). Indo-European *-i̯es-* extended by *-nis-* appears in the comparative suffix *-esnis* of Lith. *saldẽsnis* (posit. *saldùs*). The *-i̯os-* grade of this suffix is perceptible also in Skt. *náv-yas* (cf. posit. *náv-a*), and the *-i̯ōs*-grade in Old Lat. *maiōsibus* etc. (Kieckers II, p. 88.). Being formed with a primary suffix these forms are directly derived from the root, of which, as explained above, the meaning was altogether of an unspecified character, though susceptible to approximation as noun, adjective, verb, etc. A "comparative" suffix when appended to such elements can only serve to intensify the meaning. This was in fact the original function of the suffixes *-yas* and *-iṣṭha*. It is significant that for most of the forms in *-yas* and *-iṣṭha* it is impossible to point out corresponding adjectives of the positive degree, for they are derived directly from the root (*jáv-īyas, véd-īyas* : *jáv-iṣṭha, véd-iṣṭha*)—which would show that these comparatives and superlatives were not at all motivated to intensify primarily only the adjective elements in the roots (here *jū-* and *vid-*) as is usually supposed. These suffixes in fact originally served to intensify every aspect of the thought-content associated with the roots. Thus *yáj-īyas* signified "one who sacrifices particularly well" (nominal) and *vár-īyas* signified "a thing which is very wide" (adjective). That these forms were originally more substantives than adjectives is further suggested by the fact that in the Centum-languages the forms in *-ios* pass for both masculine and feminine (cf. Latin comparatives in *-ior*).

It may be noticed in passing that the weak-grade form

(*-is-*) of this suffix extended by *-on-* (*-is-on-*) became an independent comparative suffix already in the original Indo-European (cf. Gr. *hēdíon-os* <**hēd-ison-os*, Goth. *sut-iz-ins*, Lith. *sald-ēsni-s*). A trace of this *-ios-* ; *-is(o)n-* may perhaps still be found is Skt. *téj-īyas* : *tīk-ṣṇá*. This explains also the curious cross-form *tekṣṇ-iṣṭha* (TĀr. 2. 13.1) which has been always a puzzle to Sanskrit grammarians. It is in fact a double superlative. When *-s(o)n-* as a superlative suffix had become obsolete in the language the more common suffix *-iṣṭha-* had to be added to it over and above the original suffix *-s(o)n-*. The form *ak-ṣṇ-a* (>*aś-sn-a*) at the side of *áś-iṣṭha* (posit. *āś-ú*) is another example of the Indo-European comparative suffix *-son-* in Sanskrit. The intensive meaning conveyed by this suffix, which later came to be regarded as a degree of comparison, is clear also in *vadh-a-sná* "deadly weapon" as opposed to *vadh-á* "weapon".

The secondary suffixes *-tara*, *-tama*, both of Indo-European origin (cf. Gr. *-tero*, Lat. *-tumu-s* in *quot-tumus*), are hardly distinguishable in value in later Skt. from *-īyas* *-iṣṭha*, but their original meaning is still clearly perceptible in the language. The suffixes *-īyas* : *-iṣṭha* served to intensify the inherent qualities of a subject, but the function of *-tara* *-tama* was rather selective : *-tara* was used to distinguish one out of two, and *-tama* one out of many. The selective value of these suffixes comes to light particularly when they are attached to pronominal stems,—*ka-tará ka-tamá*, *anya-tará anya-tama*. Forms like *Káṇva-tama*, *nádi-tame* and *gaja-tama* (Aśoka's inscription) are understandable only in this light. Both these suffixes are doubtless compounded ones,—they are extensions by *-ra* and *-ma* of the suffix *-ta* discussed above, which appear as independent suffixes in *apa-rá apa-má* etc. Both these *-ra* and *-ma* are of Indo-European antiquity, for Latin *inter* corresponds Skt. *ánta-ra*, and the suffix *-ma* can still be traced in *pri-mu-s* of the same language.

The secondary suffix *-mant* is functionally identical and partially interchangeable with *-vant* which has been mentioned above, and the only feature distinguishing it from the latter seems to be its aversion to stems in *-a-*. This variableness of the initial element shows that it is but the participial suffix *-ant* in another form. The initial *-m-* of *-mant* might be due to the analogical influence of *-māna* discussed below. The suffix *-vant* (<*-u̯ent*) however was already used in the original Indo-European to form denominative adjectives as in Skt. (Brugm.-Th. §215). The suffix *-māna* used to form passive particles in Skt. is similarly of Indo-European origin, cf. Gr. *-meno-*. On the testimony of the Greek form of the suffix it ought to have been* *-mana* in Skt. and not *-māna*. The only way to explain this apparent anomaly is to assume the analogical influence of the corresponding participal suffix *-āna* of middle and passive value. This suffix *-āna* is at least of Indo-Iranian antiquity (cf. *stáv-āna* : Av. *stavanō*, *sunv-āná* : Av. *hunvana*), but its origin remains obscure. It might at all events have owed its origin to the participal suffix *-na* joining *ā*-stems (Bartholomae, Vorgeschichte §209, 3, f.-n. 1). A peculiar feature of this suffix is that not infrequently it is joined to the aoristic stem in *-s*, e.g. *mandasānà*, *vṛddhasāná* etc. (Whitney §897b). Bartholomae (Ibid.) gives at least one Avestan form in *-āna* derived from an *s*-aorist stem: *mərəxšānō*. Within Skt. the suffix *-āna* quickly lost ground till at last in the classical language it became a rarity.

In classical Skt. abstract nouns may be formed from almost every adjective by adding to it *-tva* or *-tā*. In the older language too both these two suffixes are used for the same purpose, though not at all so extensively. Extended forms of both are in evidence besides these simpler suffixes, —thus beside *-tā* are found *-tāt* and *-tāti*, and beside *-tva* the compound suffix *-tvana*, e. g. *devá-tāt*, *devá-tāti*, *pati-tvaná*. The suffix *-tvana* is evidently an extension by *-na* of the suffix *-tva* (MacDonell §218). But it is necessary to further divide the suffix, for the corresponding Greek form *-suno-* is derived from *-tu-na* (Brug.-Th. § 196). The suffix *-tvana* thus turns out to be *-tu-a-na*. The whole complex should have thus to be derived from *-tu-* which need not be different from the homonymous primary suffix discussed above. Nothing however can be said with certainty about the origin of, and the inter-relation between, *-tā*, *-tāt* and *-tāti*, excepting perhaps that in the last analysis they are all derived from the primary suffix *-t-* (see p. 102).

Lastly we have to consider the compounds, which, in principle, are undistinguishable from the suffix-made words discussed above. For very probably most of these suffixes, perhaps in a different form, had been independent words in the language at some time or other,—like German *-heit* (<Goth. *haidus*) and French *-ment* (<Lat. *mens mentis*) to give two well-known instances out of many. On the other hand it is equally difficult to distinguish a compound from a sentence, for in languages in which holophrasis is the rule (as in the Red Indian languages) every sentence is actually a compound in which the individual units undergo those

modifications which are characteristic of units in compounds. Later Skt. too, in which page-long compounds are not at all rare, may be said to be a holophrastic language, only with this difference that the Sanskrit of Bāṇa, Māgha and Bhāravi cannot be called a language if by it is meant a true and living medium of expression. But in the Vedic period, when Skt. was truly a living language, compounds of such inordinate length were quite unknown, and as in the Homeric language too the compounds are approximately of the same length as in the Veda (generally of two members) it may be assumed that in the Indo-European the compounds were not much different. Compared to Greek, Latin seems to be curiously poor in compounds, but that is due to the sharp expiratory accent of the language perhaps due to Etruscan influence, on account of which in words of any length the final syllables were weakened or dropped altogether, e.g. *hospes* <**hosti-potis*, *vipera* <**vīvo-parā*, etc.

The two chief characteristics of compounds are the unity of accent and the flexibility of only the last member. But none of these characteristics is absolute, for there are compounds in which both members are inflected and both are accented. The Sandhi between the components of a compound is often quite peculiar ; it is, in fact, something midway between internal and external sandhi. Moreover in compounds sometimes such stem-forms come into play as are otherwise quite unknown. The law of the unity of accent is oftenest ignored, as might be also otherwise expected, by the co-ordinative dvandva-compounds, in which each individual component preserves its independence to such a degree that sometimes each member retains even its own flexional ending. The Devatā-dvandvas and adverbial compounds such as *áhar-divá* are the well-known examples of such double-accented co-ordinatives. Double accent is unkown when the first component appears in its stem-form excepting in a few cases such as *śácī-páti*, *tánū-nápāt*, etc. The vacillating character of compositional sandhi is best proved by a number of compositions of which the first element is *dus-* : sometimes, following the law of internal sandhi, the initial dental of the second component is cerebralised and *duṣ-* becomes *dū-* (by compensatory lengthening) as in *dū-ḍábha*, *dū-ḍhí*, *dū-ṇáśa* ; but as often are found forms without such a cerebral, e. g. *dur-dṛ́śīka*, *dur-ṇáśa* etc.

The peculiar forms often seen in the first components require some consideration. Sometimes these forms are distinctly of Indo-European origin, thus *kaput-* in *kapúc-chala* (cf. Lat. *caput*). In some cases this particular form may be proved to have been in use in the original Indo-European only as the first component of compounds. This is particularly true of a number of stems in *-ra* which in composition assume an *i*-form, e. g. *śvit-rá* : *śvit-y-áñc-*. An exact parallel may be found in Gr. *argós* <**arg-rós* : *argi-kéraunos*. A similar case of the use of a special heteroclitic stem in compound is to be found in *rā́ja-putra* (stem *rā́jan-*) etc. Here the question is whether the first component *rāja-* is the weak-grade form *rājn̥-* of the stem *rājan-* or is it the direct descendant of **rājo-*. The latter alternative is suggested by the corresponding forms in other languages, cf. Gr. *akmó-theton* : *akmón*, Lat. *homi-cida* (<**homocida*) : *homōn* etc., for the *-o* of Gr. *akmo-* and Lat **homo-* cannot be derived from Indo-European *-n̥*.

The behaviour of the second member in compound is much more complex. Even apart from the various *samā-*

sāntas (compositional suffix) which often lend quite a peculiar aspect to it, the second member often appears in ablaut-forms which are otherwise quite unknown, though not unoften they are of pre-Indian antiquity. Sometimes these ablaut-forms appear also in the first component, but that perhaps through later analogical transfer. The best known examples of such peculiar ablaut-forms in the second component are those of *gó-* (>*gu*), *jā́nu* (>*jñu*), *dā́ru* (>*dru*). The compounds in *-gu* (e. g. *ádhri-gu, saptá-gu, su-gú* etc.) are at least of Indo-Iranian antiquity, cf. Old Pers. *θata-gu* (=Skt. *śata-gú*). The weak-grade form *-jñu* in the second component goes back to still earlier times, for besides Av. *ā-žnubyas* it is testified to by Gr. *gnúx*; the Skt. examples are *mitá-jñu, asita-jñú* etc. The weak-grade form *dru-* (<*dā́ru*) on the other hand appears only in the first component of quotable compounds, *dru-pad-á dru-ṇas-á* etc. A weak-grade form of the word *paśú* is perhaps concealed in the root *rapś-* abstracted out of the compound *vīra-paśu-* ! In Avestan at any rate this weak-grade form (*-fšu-*) is well attested, *e.g. haurva-fšu, fradat̰-fšu* etc.

The samāsānta suffixes are taken mostly by Bahuvrihis, and those specially favoured are *-ka, -i, -ya* and *-a*. The samāsānta *-ka* is very probably identicial in origin with the very common secondary suffix *-ka*, which is of Indo-European antiquity. But the compositional *-ka* may be easily distinguished from the suffixal *-ka*, for the former is never accented while the latter almost always is. (The accentuation in *ajāvikā́* for instance can be explained only if it is assumed that *-ka* here is a diminutive suffix attached to *avi-*). The compositional suffix *-i* of Bahuvrihi compounds is distinctly of Indo-European origin, for forms like *práty-ardhi* (: *árdha*),

dhūmá-gandhi (: *gandhá*) are paralleled by Av. ***avi-miθri*** (: *miθra*), Lat. *tri-lingu-is* (: *lingua*) etc. The samāsānta *-ya* was equally in evidence in the original Indo-European, cf. Gr. *ennéa-boios* (: *boũs*) "worth nine pieces of cattle", Lat. *acu-ped-ius* "fleet-footed", Avestan (*θri-*)*māh-ya* : Skt. (*sapta-*)*mās-ya*. Compare also Gr. *homo-gástr-ios* : Skt. *sá-garbh-ya* etc. The commonest of all the Skt. samāsāntas is of course the compositional *-a* which goes back distinctly to the original Indo-European, cf. Gr. *ó-patr-os* "having the same father," *hekatóm-ped-os* "measuring hundred feet," Avestan *urv-āp-a* "containing vast sheet of water." Gradually this samāsānta *-a* became so popular in Skt. that it often *replaced* the suffixal endings of second members, particularly of those ending in *-an* and *-i*, cf. ***viśvá-karma-***, *priyá-dhāma-* (from *kárman*, *dhā́man*) and *daśāṅgulá* (: *aṅgúri*), *pūrṇa-darvá* (: *darvī́*) etc.

After the fashion of the ancient Indian grammarians the compounds may be broadly divided into three groups : (*a*) *ubhayapadārthapradhāna* or co-ordinative compounds (dvandva) in which each member is equally independent ; (*b*) *uttarapadārthapradhāna* in which the last component rules the former, *i.e.* determinative compounds (*tatpuruṣa*, *karmadhāraya*), and (*c*) *anyapadārthapradhāna* in which the idea aimed at lies outside the sphere of concepts represented individually by the component members (*bahuvrīhi*, literally meaning "one with much rice," in which the central idea is connoted neither by "much" nor by "rice" but by "one" who is beyond both these concepts). Sanskrit compounds in these broad groups will be briefly discussed in the following.

The different stages in the development of the dvandva-compounds may be clearly perceived in the RV. as Wackernagel has pointed out :—

The oldest dvandvas are clearly those in which each member is dual in form and has a separate accent, *e.g. mitrā́-váruṇau, dyā́vā-kṣā́mā.* The relation between the components of these compounds is so loose that they often appear in the RV. and later separated from each other (*dyā́vā ha kṣā́mā, dyā́vā yajñáiḥ pṛthivī́* etc.). But if not separated from each other in this way the two components together form one whole phonologically and they combine according to the laws of internal sandhi, cf. *agnī́-ṣómau.* As for their origin, it is clear that the syntactical juxtaposition of the individual components had played a decisive part in it. There can be no reasonable doubt that the compound *mitrā́-váruṇau* came about through juxtapositions like *mitró váruṇaś ca* or *mitráś ca váruṇaś ca.* Yet such a juxtaposition cannot explain the dual ending of the first component. For that it is necessary to resort to the elliptic dual which is distinctly of Indo-European origin and clear traces of which may still be found in the RV. Thus *dyā́vā* in RV. is equivalent to *dyā́vā-pṛthivī́*, just as Gr. *Aian te* means "Aias and Teukros", and Latin *Castores* means "Castor and Pollux". Even in classical Skt. *pitarau* continued to signify "father and mother".

In the next stage, the first member of these dvandvas, although retaining its independent accent, freezes into a particular flexional form, often at variance with that of the second (i.e. of the whole compound), e.g. *mitrā́-váruṇābhyām, dyā́vā-pṛthivyóḥ* etc. The first dual in these dvandvas however began to lose its accent already in the RV., cf. *indrā-pūṣṇóḥ.* It was now necessary only to use the first component in its stem-form to get the usual dvandvas of the classical language. Only two such forms are found in the first nine maṇḍalas of RV. : *indra-vāyū́* and *satyānṛté*.

The singular dvandvas with neutral ending (samāhāra) are distinctly of later origin. As these compounds carry a collective sense their singular ending is as it should be. But the oldest example of two masculines or two feminines combining to form a neutral dvandva is in ŚB. In the oldest samāhāras the first component still shows the dual ending, *e.g. iṣṭā-pūrtám*, which suggests that there was a time when each component of even these samāhāras had its own accent—as we still find in *idhmā́-barhís* (M. S.). But *idhmā́-barhís* itself can hardly have been the original form, for as shown above, double accent generally goes with double ending. It therefore probably goes back to **idhmā́-barhíṣī* ; for *iṣṭā-pūrtám* too, accordingly, a similar urform *iṣṭā́-pūrtā́(ni)* has to be postulated.

As for the determinative tatpuruṣa compounds which are so common later in the Skt. language, it is surprising to find that they are quite rare in RV. In the earliest Greek too these compounds are not at all very popular. Yet some of them, specially those with *-pada* or *-pati* as second member, are of Indo-European antiquity (cf. Gr. *dá-pedon, dés-potēs* <**dems potēs*). The unity of accent had been as little achieved in the earliest period in these tatpuruṣas as in the dvandvas discussed above, and as in the latter, in the double-accented tatpuruṣas too the first member could take a flexional form (in this case almost always the case-form in gen. sg.), *bṛ́h-as-páti, ván-as-páti*. In *nárā-śáṃsa* (<**náram-śáṃsa*, cf. *narā́ṃ ná śáṃsa* RV. 1.173,9) we find still traces of a plural ending in the first member of a tatpuruṣa compound. The retention of other than genitive case-ending in the first component of tatpuruṣas is rare, *e.g.* *vācā́-stena* (Instr.), *dā́syave-vṛ̥ka* (Dat.), *apsu-ṣomá* (Loc.).

Still less frequent in the older literature are the determinatives of which the first member is an adjective (karmadhāraya !). The oldest examples are, *eka-vīrá*, *candrá-mā̆s* "bright moon", *mahā-dhaná* etc. In a large number of older Karmadhārayas however a preposition appears as the first component. Some at least of these preverbial first components are of Indo-European antiquity,—particularly *pra-*, cf. *prá-napāt* : Lat. *pro-nepōs*. The preverbs thus employed usually retain their original meanings in these compounds. In a small group closely allied to them a finite verb-form appears as the first component, e. g. *trasá-dasyu*, *śikṣā-nará*, *radā-vasu* (rhythmic lengthening of the final vowel in *śikṣā-*, *radā-*), in which the first components are nothing but forms in 2. sg. imperative. However unusual, this type is distinctly of Indo-European antiquity, cf. Gr. *pheré-oikos* "carrying home", *arché-kakos* "causing evil" etc. A fine parallel to these forms may be found in modern French *rendez-vous*. Equally old is another group in which the first component, though not a verb-form, has an active verbal force, *e.g.*, *dā́ti-vāra* "giving riches" *vīti-hotra* "enjoying the sacrifice" etc.—which are paralleled by Gr. *bōti-áneira* "feeding men" etc. (Wackernagel II, 1, p. 320).

In contrast to the Tatpuruṣas and Karmadhārayas the Bahuvrihis are exocentric in meaning (Pāṇ. 2. 2. 24 : *anya-padārthe*). But for the fact that in the older language they are much more frequent than the former, it might be said that the Bahuvrihis are adjectivised Karmadhārayas distinguished only by the accent,—the Brahuvrīhis generally take the accent on the first component and the Karmadhārayas on the second. Patañjali has shown, quoting a well-known story, what a disaster may follow from confusing the accent of homonymous Bahuvrīhis and Tatpuruṣas. The origin of Bahuvrīhi compounds is one of the most discussed problems of Comparative Philology, but a concensus of opinion on this point has not been reached. Wackernagel at all events has ingeniously suggested that they are probably derived from original paratactical constructions, thus *nárah sv-áśvāḥ* from **néres su-ekuōs* is derived from still older **néres su ekuōs* in which every member is an independent entity. In the same way, *indrajyeṣṭhā devā́ḥ* presupposes a construction like "*devā́ḥ indro jyéṣṭhaḥ*". What lends welcome support to Wackernagel's theory is the fact that similar paratactical constructions are actually found, *e.g.* RV. 1,130,8 : *tvácaṃ kṛṣṇā́m arandhayat* "he delivered the black skin. (*i.e.* those having a black skin)"; 1,114,5 : *varāháṃ......tveṣáṃ rūpám* "the boar, the ruddy colour" (*i.e.* the ruddy-coloured boar"). Similar loose paratactical constructions are found also in other languages, thus Lat. *urbs antiqua fuit, Tyrii tenuere coloni, Karthago* (Aeneis 1, 12) "there was an ancient city named Carthage, Tyrian colonists held".—Bahuvrīhis are quite common also in the oldest Greek, cf. *rhododáktylos* "rosy-fingered," "*ōkú-pteros* "fleet-winged" etc. As in Vedic, in the oldest Greek too, they are much more numerous than the Karmadhārayas.

SANSKRIT NOUN-INFLEXION.

In the field of morphology the first thing that strikes us in the Ṛgvedic language is the considerable amount of mobility exhibited by endings and suffixes which sometimes produce the illusion of presenting the very process of agglutination by which the Indo-European flexional systems in general have been developed. In quite a number of cases in the Ṛgveda the ending of a stem has evidently to be supplied from a form standing in apposition to it. Thus *návyasā vácas* for *návyasā vácasā*, *tṛ́ṣu rocané* for *tṛ́ṣu rocanéṣu*, etc. In these cases the ending has been actually treated like the second member of a compound. A similar state of things is indicated by a number of cases in the Vedic dialect in which a case-ending alternates with an adverbial suffix : cf. RV. 6, 18, 9 *hásta ā́ dakṣiṇatrā́*. Here the locative suffix *-tra* evidently functions for the locative ending *-e* of *háste*. In the same way in passages like *tátaḥ ṣaṣṭhā́d ā́ 'mútaḥ* (AV. 8, 9, 6) the ablative suffix *-taḥ* (cf. Pāṇini's *pañcamyās tasil*) is equivalent to the ablative ending *-āt* in *ṣaṣṭhā́t*. These and similar examples in Skt. and other Indo-European languages are however too few in number and always exposed to the suspicion of being sporadical products of poets' caprices, and are therefore unable to justify the conclusion, sometimes put forward, that the Vedic dialect still shows traces of a pre-flexional stage. We have to assume that like all other Indo-European dialects Sanskrit too presupposes a fully developed and well-established flexional system.

In curious contrast to the multifarious innovations in the field of phonology described above, Sanskrit has preserved the original Indo-European case-system with remarkable fidelity. There is no reason to believe that the Indo-European case-system differed materially from that of Sanskrit. Both nominal and pronominal flexional systems in Sanskrit have preserved their distinctive features till Sanskrit had long ceased to be a living language, and the only serious case of syncretism is to be found in the use of dative for genitive from the Brāhmaṇas onwards, which is clearly due to syntactical reasons. Yet it is almost certain that Sanskrit instrumental combines in itself two different cases—those of accompaniment and means respectively, and that the two very different modes of forming instrumental plural (in *-aiḥ* and *-bhiḥ*) reflect the previous existence of two different cases which were combined in the historical period into the Sanskrit instrumental.

Yet a comparative and historical study of Sanskrit morphology clearly reveals the process by which this apparently fixed and rigid flexional system was developed. Let us begin with the ending *-su* in loc. pl. This ending is undoubtedly of Indo-European origin, as is proved by the corresponding Avestan ending *-hu* and Old Ch. Sl. ending *-chŭ**. But we have to take into account also the ending *-si* in dat. pl. in Greek, for it is nothing but the original locative ending functioning in the dative. The ending *-si* in Greek shows that the original Indo-European ending was *-s-* alone, which was later strengthened by different deictic particles in different languages, by *-i-* in

* It is important to note however that both these two languages belong to the *Satəm* group.

Greek, and by *-u-* in Sanskrit, Avestan and Old Ch. Sl. Thurneysen ingeniously suggested that the deictic particles *i* and *u* were used to strengthen the original ending *-s-* to indicate nearness and distance respectively, but later in one group the particle *i* came to be used also to indicate distant objects, and in another the particle *u* usurped the function of *i*. There can be hardly any doubt that Thurneysen has given the right explanation of the origin of the Indo-European ending in loc. pl., for locative is the case *par excellence* in which an emphatic deictic particle may be expected, and its subsequent history in the individual Indo-European dialects also shows that similar strengthening particles or post-positions had been actually added to its endings. In RV. the post-position *ā́* is often used after locatives in expressions like "*dámeṣv ā́*" "in the houses", but in Skt. this post-position had never become an integral part of the ending. This step had however been achieved in Avestan, where the ending in loc. pl. is not only *-hu*, *-šu*, but also *-hvă*, *-švă* sometimes. In Old Persian this ending in loc. plur. is never without the post-position *ā*.

The important innovations of Skt. with regard to the ending for gen. pl., mostly in common with Avestan, have been already discussed in Chapter II. But here too the Ṛgvedic language shows some peculiarities which distinguish it not only from other Indo-European languages, but also from classical Skt. In several passages of the RV. forms in *-īn*, *-ūn*, *-ṝn* have been evidently used in gen. pl. Here the real genitive ending *-ām* has been altogether dispensed with. But these forms are very probably due to mechanical form-analogy and no special linguistic value should be attached to them. We have seen that besides the usual form *devā́nām* the RV. also knows *devā́m* in gen. pl., which in Sandhi (cf. *devā́ñ jánma*) may further appear to be nothing but *devā́n*. Now, on the analogy of this **devā́n* beside *devā́nām* the Ṛgvedic poets might have further constructed *nṝ'n* for the usual *nṝ'ṇām*. These shorter forms are therefore purely momentary formations devoid of any historical value. The same applies also to the form *ūtī́* (from *ūti*) in instr. pl., which is several times distinctly qualified by adjectives ending in *-bhis* (e. g. *ugrébhir ūtī́*).

No case however shows such a rich variety of forms in plural as the nom.-accusative of neuter stems. The ending in this case was in fact originally a singular one, for the plurality of neuter objects* used to be conceived generally in the collective sense—as *one* collection of neuter objects. A truly plural ending was regularly used when this collective sense was absent. Already in the Ṛgvedic language however this sharp distinction between collective and distributive plurals could no longer be maintained. Therefore we find here all sorts of singular endings applied to neuter stems in nom.-acc. pl.

In classical Skt. the nom.-acc. pl. neuter is uniformly characterised by the ending *-i*, which is accompanied by a nasal element following immediately after vowel-stems : *e.g.* *-ā-ni*, *-ī-ni*, *-ū-ni*, *-ṝ-ṇi* (Type I) ; in the case of consonant-stems containing a nasal in the final element the ending is merely *-i*, *e.g.* *-ān-i*, *-añc-i*, *-ant-i* (Type II) ; but where there is no nasal preceding the final consonant of the stem the ending *-i* is strengthened by a nasal coming immediately *before* the final consonant, *e.g.* *-āṃsi*, *-īṃsi*, *-ūṃsi* (Type III) ;

* To a lesser extent also of nouns of other genders.

the radical stems formally belong to the last group, *e.g.* *-śak* : *-śaṅk-i*, *-yuj* : *-yuñj-i* (Type IV).

The Vedic language however reveals a state of things which is altogether different. Beside Type I there are forms in *-ā*, *-ī*, *-ū* without the characteristic ending *-ni* ; the *an*-stems of Type II show the ending *-ā* beside *-āni*. Type III has been fully developed there already, but there is no trace as yet of Type IV. In fact, so far as the older language is concerned, the forms in question may be divided into two broad groups : (1) Consonant-stems using the ending *-i*, *e.g.* *catvā́r-i*, *-an-i* (*an*-stems), *-ănt-i* etc., and (2) Vowel-stems merely lengthening the final vowel without taking any ending at all (*-ā*, *-ī*, *-ū*), though however the final vowel may also appear in its original short form (*-i*, *-u*). Beside the forms in *-ā -ī -ū* we find already in the older language those in *-āni*, *-īni*, *-ūni* from vowel-stems—the only ones current in classical Skt. But the latter are doubtless later analogy-formations, for no trace of them can be found in the allied languages.

The ending *-i* in nom.-acc. pl. neut. of consonant-stems is met with also in Avestan : cf. *nāmən-i* = Skt. *nā́mān-i*. In other Indo-European languages the corresponding ending is *-a*, cf. Gr. *onómata*, Lat. *nomina*, Goth. *namna*. This shows that the original Indo-European ending was *-ə*. The characteristic nasal infix associated with it, excepting in *catvā́r-i*, must have been derived from those cases where a nasal was already present in the stem (*e.g.* *nt-* and *ñc*-stems). Thus the participial stem *sant-* appeared as *sát* (<*sn̥t*) in sg., but in plural it was *sā́nti* ; similarly *ghṛtávat* : *ghṛtávānti*, *paśumát* : *paśumā́nti*.* On the basis of these forms

* These forms with long penultimate vowel at the side of short-vowel ones

an infixed nasal came to be regarded as an essential feature of nom.-acc. pl. neut. of consonant-stems, and gradually it was introduced also into radical stems (*yuj-* : *yuñji*, *vṛt-* : *vṛnti* etc.) in post-Ṛgvedic language, although here such a nasal has no etymological justification.

As for vowel-stems, the ending *-āni* of *a*-stems, unknown in Indo-European and Indo-Iranian periods, is derived from *-an*-stems. The *a*-stems naturally drew after them also the *i-* and *u*-stems and gave rise to the endings *-īni*, *-ūni*. But the element *-ni* is anything but constant in these endings in the Ṛgvedic language. In fact forms in *-ā*, *-ī*, *-ū* are here as much in evidence as those in *-āni*, *-īni*, *-ūni*, and the evidence of cognate languages proves that these shorter endings are the old and original ones.

What is the origin of the endings *-ī*, *-ū*? They may be the result of contraction of the Indo-European ending *-ə*, revealed by consonant-stems (see above), with the final vowel *i*, *u* of the stem. Thus *purū́* in nom.-acc. pl. ntr. is derived from *purú + ə*, and *apratī́* in same position is nothing but *aprati + ə*. In this way, the curious shorter endings are brought into harmony with the original Indo-European on the one hand, and on the other, forms like *catvā́r-i* are delivered from curious isolation in the midst of forms in nom.-acc. pl. neuter.

But the explanation of the short ending *-i*, *-u* in nom.-acc. neut. pl. has to be sought elsewhere. These forms are

came early to be regarded as anomalous. In the Padapāṭha therefore they are represented as *santi*, *ghṛtavanti*, *paśumanti* etc. But the length of the penultimate was respected also in the Padapāṭha where the penultimate was long in the corresponding masculine form; thus *mahānti* also in Pp. on the analogy of *mahāntaḥ* (masc.)

truly without any ending at all, and they are precious relics of much earlier times when the inflexion of neuter stems had not yet been fully developed. Formantically they are identical with the corresponding singular forms, and that genetically too they are to be traced to the same source is proved by the fact that no short-vowel form in nom.-acc. pl. can be found in those cases where the singular form ends with a long vowel (e.g. *śīrṣā́, trī́*). The same phenomenon moreover excludes the possibility that the short-vowel forms owe their origin to rhythmic shortening of the long-vowel ones, as might be otherwise argued on the ground of instances like *urū́ vár̥āṃsi* (RV. 10, 89, 2) but *urú jyótīṃṣi* (RV. 9, 91, 6),—long vowel before a simple consonant, but short vowel before a consonant-group. Neither can these forms be regarded merely as collective singulars, for that would be to ignore the difficulty of the Ṛgvedic composers who found themselves without any linguistic tradition regarding most of these neuter stems. What would be the plural of *ū́dhar* for instance? The Ṛṣis in these cases did not hesitate to use the singular form also in plural, cf. *ū́dhar divyā́ni* (RV. 1, 64, 5). Yet it need not be denied that the analogy of collective singulars might have helped in setting down these singular forms also in plural, as is strongly suggested by the juxtaposition of collective singular and endingless plural as in RV. 8, 25, 17 *mitrásya vratā́* (collective singular) *váruṇasya dīrghaśrút* (endingless plural).

The ending *-i* is very much in evidence also in the *singular* of neuter consonant stems, cf. *hā́rd-i* from *hr̥d-*. This *-i* however is not derived from Indo-European *ə* like the same ending in plural, for in the non-Indo-Iranian languages an *-i* (not *-ā*) corresponds to it, cf. *hā́rd-i* : Gr. *kardía*, Lith. *širdis*. Already at a very early date this light ending came to be regarded as part of the stem ; thus the stem *vār-* of the older language later assumed the form *vāri-* by completely incorporating the original ending *-i*. The same is the case also with *ákṣi*, *ásthi*, *sákthi* etc. In the later language they are all regarded as anomalous *i*-stems, sometimes substituting the final *-i* by *-an*. But there is abundant internal and external evidence to prove that originally they were all consonant-stems. For *akṣi-* the necessary proof is furnished by the form *an-ák* (<**an-akṣ*) in RV., and Avestan *ast-* and Latin *oss-* prove that *asthi-* too is derived from the consonant stem **asth-*. Not wholly dissimilar is the case of the stem *van-* "tree" which has been thematised into *vana-* already in the Vedic period. The original consonant-stem is clearly perceptible in *van-ā́m* (gen. pl.), *váṃ-su* (loc. pl.) etc. But the heteroctitic *ar*-stem *vanar-* is clearly in evidence at its side not only in *vanar-gú vanar-ṣád*, but also perhaps in the nominal derivative *vā́nar-a* "monkey". The original stem extended by *-an* has given rise to the forms *vánan-vatī* etc.

To a still earlier state of things point a number of striking cases in which, unlike *van-* : *vanar-*, where the original stem may be said to have been extended by *-ar*, the latter evidently acts as a locative case-suffix. Thus from the pronominal stem *ta-* we have on the one hand *tá-d* and on the other *tá-r(-hi)*. This interchange of suffixes is of Indo-European antiquity, for English *that* and *there* exactly correspond to these Skt. terms not only in form but in meaning as well. In the compound *áhar-divi* therefore the form *áhar-* may be regarded as a locative of the type **ta-r* in *tár-hi*. Similarly *uṣar-* in *uṣar-búdh-* may be the loc. sg. of a stem **uṣ-* of which *uṣā́* is but the form in instr. sg.

But beside this *-ar*, a locative suffix *-an* was in existence already from pre-Indian times, cf. Skt. *jmán* but Av. *zəmarə*, both meaning "on the earth". It is evidently this *-an* which we find in the oblique cases of *ákṣi*, *ásthi* etc., as well as in those of neuter stems showing the characteristic *r* in nom.-acc. sg. (e.g. *áhar*, *yákṛt*). It is permissible to guess that this ending *-an* in loc. sg. is one of the causes of the continued endinglessness of *an*-stems in that position : in forms like *nā́man*, *dhánvan* the element *-an* itself came to be regarded as ending as in *jmán*, and therefore no further ending was added to them in loc. sg.

It hardly needs to be pointed out that the elements *-ar*, *-an* are not mere case-endings in the ordinary sense. They rather show how the system of case-endings has gradually developed. They are adverbial particles attached to noun-stems indicating their relation to particular verb-forms or, as in the case of genitive, to other noun-stems.

The *n*-flexion of neuter *i*, *u*-stems may be discussed in this connection. They received the nasal element in nom.-acc. pl. from *n*-stems as explained above. But what is the origin of the *-n-* of other cases ? First of all we have to note that its origin must have been different from that of *-inā*, *-unā* of masculine *i*, *u*-stems. For, as Wackernagel argues, in masculine, *-inā* and *-unā* are equally in evidence in RV., whereas the *-in*-forms of *i*-neuters are negligible in comparison with the neuter *-un*-forms. The masculine *-inā*, *-unā* beside older *-(i)yā*, *-(u)vā* may be explained simply by the analogy of *in*-stems ; *bali-bhiḥ* : *balin-ā* = *agni-bhiḥ* : *agni-nā*. But for the *n*-flexion of *-i -u*-neuters it is necessary to look back much farther. The very fact that *-un*-forms are abundant and *-in*-forms rare in RV. shows that the origin of this *n*-flexion has to be sought in some characteristic feature of the neuter *u*-stems. Now, it is a peculiar feature of some of these *u*-stems that already in the Indo-European period they had at their side alternating heteroclitic stems in *n*. Thus Skt. *dā́ru* seems to have had a stem **doruṇ-* (cf. Gr. *dorvat*) at its side. This *n* was gradually extended to dative, ablative etc., specially when an *n* became a fixed element in nom.-acc. pl. of these stems. The neuter *an*-stems must have been of decisive importance in this respect, for their vowel ending *-a* in nom.-acc. sg. as opposed to *-nā*, *-naḥ*, *-ni* etc. in other cases presented a convenient model for the growth of similar nasal endings for neuter *-i*, *-u*-stems.

The characteristic ending in loc. sg. is *-i*, which was originally doubtless a local post-position. The *a*-stems of Skt. know only the ending *-e* in loc. sg., which is, of course, *-a+i*, as is proved also by other languages, cf. *e.g.* Gr. *oiko-i* (:*oiko-s*). For other vowel-stems, however, this *-i* is anything but certain, and the same applies to the consonant-stems. There are important groups of stems which take no ending at all in loc. sg. Endingless forms are attested by the *u*-stems (as well as *i*-stems which took over the ending of the latter) and the *Vṛkī*-flexion (see below) of *ī*-stems, but most clearly by the *an*-stems, in whose case other languages prove its hoary antiquity. Besides, there are some isolated forms of other consonant-stems which look like endingless locatives. Such are, for instance, the stems in *-ar*. But the forms in question, *e.g.* *áhar* (and *ū́dhar* !), may be regarded as simple adverbs like *svàr*. In fact, all endingless locatives were mere adverbs originally, and as an adverbial force is inherent in every locative, it is not too much to think that all locatives had once been endingless. The post-position *-i* however came to be used in it at a very early date to obtain clear, unequivocal forms, but continued to be dispensed with by those stems which assumed distinctive forms in this position (cf. *-au* of *u-* and *i*-stems). The *Vṛkī*-stems too could dispense with an ending in loc. sg., because they had a distinctive sigmatic form in nom. sg. which the *Devī*-stems lacked. Only the *an*-stems, which assumed no striking form in loc. sg. carried on without any ending till a comparatively late period. It is tempting to suggest that the analogy of *-ar* : *-an*-stems had been the cause of the continued endinglessness of locatives of *an*-stems. The form *áhan** in loc. sg. was so markedly distinguished from *áhar* (nom.-acc. sg.) that it could do without any specific ending at all, and once *áhan* came to be recognised as loc. sg. it naturally drew after it also *nā́man, dhánvan* etc. which had no alternating *r*-form in nom.-acc. As the *r/n*-stems are of Indo-European origin the endingless locatives of *n*-stems in other languages (cf. Gr. *aiēn*, loc. sg. to *aiṓn*, etc.) may also be explained in this way.

Besides the stems in *-an* those in *-ū* too frequently exhibit endingless forms in loc. sg., cf. *camū́, tanū́*. No extra-Indian parallels to these forms can be found, unless Lat. *domū* is regarded as an old endingless locative. It is therefore better to regard them as mechanical analogy-formations after the endings *-e* : *-eṣu* of *a*-stems ; in other words, after *damé* : *daméṣu* was formed a *camū́* to *camū́ṣu*. The same explanation may be resorted to also in the case of endingless

* Beside which also the form *áh(a)ni* is known.

locative singulars of *ī*-stems of the *Vṛkī*-type (*e.g. gaurī, nadī*) though here too Latin forms like *rūrī* might be adduced to prove their Indo-European antiquity.

The endings in instrumental are varied and interesting enough in the Veda to deserve a special mention. As Wackernagel (III § 73a) summarises it, the *i*- *u*-stems have three different endings in instr. sg.: (1) -*ī* -(*ū*), (2) -(*i*)*yā* -(*u*)*vā*, (3) -*inā* -*unā*. The classical language has altogether given up the ending -*ī* (-*ū*) and the endings -(*i*)*ya* -(*u*)*vā* are confined in it only to feminine stems, so that masculine and neuter stems have in the classical language only -*inā* -*unā*, and the feminine stems only -*yā* -*vā*. In the RV. however the ending -*ī* is much more in evidence than -(*i*)*nā*, but the existence of the analogous ending -*ū* can only be inferred from its currency in the Avesta.

The oldest endings are here obviously -*ī* -*ū*, though it remains hazardous to claim for them a pre-Indo-Iranian antiquity. If both these analogous endings are to be covered by one hypothesis it would be best to imagine a suffix -*ə* which combined with -*i* and -*u* of the stem had given rise to the endings -*ī* -*ū*. There is however hardly any doubt on the point that the endings -(*i*)*yā* -(*u*)*vā* are derived from the *flexion forte* (see below). The problem in their case is to explain why and how they gradually came to be confined to feminine stems alone. But a satisfactory explanation is not far to seek. The ending -*yā* was formally identical with the ending in instr. sg. of *ī*-stems which are *feminine*; hence through the analogical influence of the latter the ending -*yā* gravitated towards the *feminine i*-stems to the exclusion of masculine and neuter ones. Thus when feminine *i*-stems were identified with the ending -*yā* in instr. sg. the corresponding feminine *u*-stems monopolised the ending *-vā*. With the progressive identification of *-yā -vā* with the feminine stems there arose the necessity of providing a new ending in instr. sg. for masculine and neuter *i-*, *u-* stems. This new ending was *-nā*, perhaps abstracted out of *in-*stems as mentioned above.

The *a*-stems in Skt. take various peculiar endings. In instr. sg. the ending is *-ena* in the classical language. This is current already in the RV., but beside it is found also the ending *-ā* (e g. *sánā* from *sana-*). As the Avestan *a*-stems take only this short ending *-ā*, this is clearly the old and original ending of *a*-stems in instr. sg. The ending *-ena* is derived from pronominal flexion. The Avesta knows an instr. sg. ending *-na* only in the case of pronouns, but no clear trace of it can be found farther back. In dat. sg. the *a*-stems in Skt. have the ending *-āya*, to which corresponds Av. *-āi*, Gr. *-ōi* etc. This shows that the original ending has been strengthened by the post-position *-a* in Skt. The ending *-āt* in abl. sg. is distinctly of Indo-European antiquity (cf. old Latin *Gnaivōd* from *Gnaivos*), and such is also the ending *-asya* in gen. sg. (cf. Homeric *-oio* <*-*osi̯o*). In plural only the instrumental endings deserve special mention. Of the two endings *-ebhiḥ* and *-aiḥ* the former as a nominal ending is a peculiarity of Skt. alone. Its pronominal origin is suggested among other things by the element *-e-* in *-ebhiḥ* (and *-ebhyaḥ*), for just as the initial *-ā-* in *-ābhyām* is nothing but the ending in dual (see below), in the same way the initial *-e* in *-ebhiḥ* and *-ebhyaḥ* is actually an ending in plural. (The ending *-e* in plural is a typical characteristic of the pronominal flexion, cf. *sárvaḥ* : *sárve*). The nominal ending *-aiḥ* on the other hand is well attested in other Indo-

European languages, cf. Gr. *-ois*, Lat. *-ois*, Lith. *-aĩs* etc. The struggle for existence between these two endings *-ebhiḥ* and *-aiḥ* is one of the most interesting chapters in Vedic grammar. In RV. *-ebhiḥ* and *-aiḥ* are equally frequent, but in AV. the forms in *-ebhiḥ* are only one-fifth of those in *-aiḥ*, and in the prose portions of TS. there is no longer any *-ebhiḥ*.

Already in its earliest stage Skt. had gone farther than any other Indo-European language in distinguishing between the inflexions of masculine and feminine nouns of similar categories by providing new endings for the latter, and this distinction has been nowhere so clearly achieved as in acc. pl. Here we find in feminine the new endings *-īḥ*, *-ūḥ*, *-ṝḥ* at the side of the older endings *-īn*, *-ūn*, *-ṝn*, which, on the evidence of other Indo-European languages, were originally used also in feminine. As in so many other similar cases, the influence of *a*-stems, which got the preponderance in Skt. as the result of Indo-European *e* and *o* coinciding with it, is the cause of this new development in Skt. Masculine and feminine endings were here actually different in the case of *o*-stems (= Skt. *a*-stems in masc. and *ā*-stems in fem.) in the original Indo-European. The Indo-European masculine *o*-stems took the ending *-ns* in acc. plur. as is proved by *-āṃs* (Sandhi-form of *-ān*) of Skt., *-ons* of Greek (Cretan) and *-ans* of Gothic. In the Indo-European epoch the corresponding ending of their feminine counterparts, the *ā*-stems, was however without any nasal element, thus sharply distinguishing the masculine forms from the corresponding feminine ones (cf. Gr. *-ās*, Goth. *-ōs*). But there was no such separate feminine ending for *-i*, *-u* and *-ṛ*-stems, and the endings *-īn(s)*, *-ūn(s)*, *-ṝn(s)* were applied there also in feminine. It was reserved for Skt. alone to replace them by *-īḥ*, *-ūḥ*, *-ṝḥ* in feminine on the analogy of *-ān* : *-āḥ* of Indo-European *o-* and *ā*-stems respectively.

It is a remarkable innovation of Skt. that a special ending *-ām* is adopted in it by various feminine stems in loc. sg. Already in the RV. it is the normal ending of *ā-* and *ī*-stems (*-āyām*, *-(i)yām*) as well as of feminine *i-* and *u*-stems. The Iranian counterpart of this *-ām* is *-ā*, which serves there to strengthen the Indo-European ending *-āi* (*i.e.* *-ā+i*) of *ā*-stems, thus giving rise to the Avestan *-āyā*, and it is certainly connected with the *-e* of Lithuanian loc. sg. ending *-oj-e* of Indo-European *ā*-stems. The Iranian *-ā* like the Lithuanian *-e* is evidently nothing but a locative post-position. The Iranian *-āyā* was further extended by the particle *-am* in Skt. and thus resulted in *-āyām* in this language, just as Iranian *-byă* strengthened by the same particle gave rise to Skt. *-bhyām*. After *-āyām* was formed analogically *-(i)yām* in loc. sg., and eventually *-(u)vām*, which however appears for the first time in AV. Instead of the latter the RV. shows the ending *-avi* (cf. *sắnavi*, *ánavi* from *sắnu*, *ánu*). As full-grade forms are to be expected in loc. sg. this *-avi* (<Indo-European **eu̯-i*) may be regarded as the original ending of *u*-stems. Yet its complete absence in Iranian might suggest that it was invented independently in Skt.

The forms in dual are remarkable for their lack of variety, for generally only three different forms are found for the eight cases. Even these few forms do not yet seem to have been permanently fixed to particular cases in the older language: the dual ending *-oḥ* is generally attributed to gen.-loc., but in the oldest part of the RV. it appears also in the ablative. *En revanche*, the ending *-bhyām* appears in the ablative for the first time in the tenth Maṇḍala. The position of the ablative dual is thus curiously uncertain. It is not even possible to say whether it originally coincided with instr.-dat. or gen.-loc. (Wackernagel III § 22a). The ending in nom.-acc. is generally ***-au***, which is of Indo-European origin, cf. Goth *aht-au* : Skt. ***aṣṭ-áu***. Very frequently however the ending is simply *-ā*, which is but a phonetic variant of *-au*. Linguistically important is the ending ***-a*** in dual preserved in the first component of the compound ***mātara-pitarau*** which has its counter-part in the Greek dual *mētére* (Wack. III§ 18e). The ending ***-bhyām*** usually comes, not after the stem, but after the flexional form in nom.-acc. dual, cf. *-ābhyām* of *a*-stems, *akṣí-bhyām* from *akṣ-í*. This is distinctly a relic from the past, for in other languages too the ending corresponding to Skt. ***-bhyām*** is attached to the form in nom.-acc. dual (Wackernagel, III §21 b *β*, p. 54). It may be concluded therefore that in the Indo-European epoch the dual had not yet been given the full status of a distinct grammatical number. The plural has a distinct sign in *s* which is almost always attached to case-forms in plural, but the dual is in principle undistinguishable from the singular.

Before concluding our treatment of the nominal flexion it is necessary to briefly discuss some of the important stem-types in Sanskrit which, again, essentially continue the Indo-European tradition.

Theoretically, stems should assume different forms according as the accent remains on it or is shifted to the ending. This is however nowhere the case*, for it is quite understandable that various stems could not be allowed

*** excepting in *sántya(voc.): satyá*.**

within one and the same system of paradigms. Yet the formantic part of the stems in question often underwent far-reaching changes as a result of the shifting of accent and this is nowhere so clear as in the case of the neuter *-añc*-stems, cf. *praty-ák :pratī-c-ī́ :praty-áñc-i*. Quite a different situation arose, however, when stems of the same type had the accent sometimes on final and sometimes on initial syllables, for the result of contraction with the case-endings could not have been identical under such circumstances. It is evidently for this reason that *ávi* and *matí* assume such dissimilar forms as *ávyaḥ* and *matéḥ* respectively in gen. sg., and among *u*-stems too we find the same contrast due to original difference in the place of accent in *krátvaḥ* and *sūnóḥ* from *krátu* and *sūnú* respectively. We find therefore two very different systems in the inflexion of *i*- *u*-stems in the older language. Beside the system of inflexion of *i*- *u*-stems current in classical Skt. the RV.—but only RV.—knows another called *flexion forte* by Saussure, which, on the evidence of cognate languages, must have been of Indo-European origin. But already in the Ṛgvedic period this *flexion forte* of *i*- *u*-stems had been almost eliminated from the language, for only 2 *i*-stems and 8 *u*-stems still show distinct traces of this flexion in it, thus *paśvā́* (nom. du.), *páśve* (dat. sg.), *paśváḥ* (gen.-abl. sg., acc. pl.), *aryáḥ* (gen.-abl. sg., nom.-acc. pl.) etc. Indo-European origin of this *flexion forte* is proved by exact parallels in other languages : acc. pl. *paśváḥ* = Avestan *pasvō*, gen. sg. *krátvaḥ* = Avestan *xraθwō* ; cf. further Greek *gounós* <**γονυός* from *gónu*-. In most cases however this *flexion forte* could provide no special distinctive forms. It is no wonder therefore that it died out at a very early date. Only the word *páti* continued to follow the *flexion forte* in some cases till into classical Skt.

A similar double flexion is found also in the case of *ī*-stems in the Veda. In their case however the stem-form in its fullest grade has to be kept much more in mind than in the case of other stems, for otherwise the inter-relation between the various forms within the system of paradigms cannot be understood at all. Historically considered, all *ī*-stems are in fact I.-E. *i̯ā*-stems, Skt. *devī́* being derived from I.-E. **deu̯ei̯ā* : **deu̯i̯ā*. In its weakest grade this base would be *devī-* (<**deu̯i̯ə*), after which is named the whole system of paradigms in Skt. But the full-grade forms make their appearance in strong cases, cf. *devyā́i*, *devyā́ḥ* etc.

Now in the case of these *ī*-stems too the duality in flexion is perhaps due to the place of accent in the original unspecified (masculine) base. The oxytonous *ī*-stems have sometimes to shift the accent from a previous syllable (*vṛ́ka* : *vṛkī́*), but where the original masculine form too was oxytonous no such shifting was necessary (*devá* : *devī́*). Now according as the accent on final *-ī* had been shifted to it from a previous syllable or not the feminine *ī*-stems exhibit two very different modes of flexion which are called *vṛkī*-flexion and *devī*-flexion respectively, after the two types mentioned above. In the Ṛgvedic language these two flexions are still sharply distinguished from each other, but the general tendency of the language has been naturally to obliterate all distinction between them, though however absolute identity of the two flexions had never been achieved in the language. Already in the RV. we find *ī*-stems which, according to origin, ought to have adopted the *devī*-flexion, often following the *vṛkī*-type, and *vice versa*.

The endings of *devī*-stems are curiously analogous to those of *ā*-stems in nom. and acc. This might be due to early influence of the *ā*-stems. Thus

	Sg.	Du.	Pl.
Nom.	*devī́*	*devī́*	*devī́ḥ*
Acc.	*devī́m*	*devī́*	*devī́ḥ*

However impracticable such a flexion might appear, being without specific forms in many cases, it is undoubtedly of Indo-European origin, for clear parallels are found in other languages. Thus the dual form in *-ī* may be found in Avestan *hamōistrī*, Lith. *vežantì* and Old Ch. Sl. *veząsti*. The weak-grade stem-form in *-ī* reigns supreme in nom. and acc. In other oblique cases too this weak-grade form is preponderant, but in the singular of instrumental, dative, abl.-gen. and loc., the stem appears in its full-grade form in *-yā*, cf. *devyā́*, *devyái*, *devyā́ḥ*, *devyā́m*. Other cognate languages too show similar strong forms in similar positions. To *devyā́* corresponds Avestan *vaŋhuyå*; to *devyái* Avestan *vaŋhuyāi*, Gr. *miāi*, Goth. *frijondjai*; to *devyā́ḥ* Avestan *vaŋhuyå*, Gr. *miās*, Goth. *frijondjōs*; and *devyā́m* has its exact parallel in Old Persian' *Harauvatiyā*. In the dual and plural of other oblique cases is again found the weak stem-form in *-ī*, —not only in Skt. but also in other Indo-European languages.

The fixity of accent is the characteristic feature of *vṛkī*-flexion. The accent in it always remains on the final *-ī* of the stem. This *-ī* however often becomes *y* in sandhi with the case-endings, with the result that the form in question gets the svarita-accent. In fact, the svarita-accent is a ready indicator of *vṛkī*-flexion. The endings too are here more like those of consonant-stems. Thus in acc. sg. a *vṛkī*-stem takes the ending *-am* (instead of *-m* of *devī*-flexion), e.g. *vṛkyàm*. Similarly *vṛkyā̀*, *vṛkyè* etc. Unlike *devī*-flexion its nom. sg. is sigmatic, e.g. *vṛkī́ḥ*. But the most curious thing about it is its loc. sg. which is without any ending at all, e.g. *gaurī́*, *nadī́*, *sarasī́*. Extra-Indian parallels to *vṛkī*-flexion are rare and uncertain. A sigmatic nom. sg. is at all events attested by Old Norse *ylgr* (<**vḷkī́s*).

In the post-Ṛgvedic literature *devī-* and *vṛkī*-flexion get mixed up more and more, until in the classical language *one* well nigh homogeneous flexional system was evolved out of a mixture of the two. On the whole the *devī*-flexion got the lion's share in this new homogeneous system, the *vṛkī*-flexion being requisitioned to supply only those forms which were not distinctive enough in the *devī*-flexion, e.g. in nom.-acc. dual and nom. pl. The nom. sg. remained a bone of contention between the two types for all time to come, and even Pāṇini and his commentators were at a loss to know where it would be sigmatic and where not.

Sanskrit pronominal flexion, specially the flexion of pronouns *par excellence*—the personal pronouns, is altogether different from nominal flexion. In the nominal flexion, as we have seen above, the stems on the whole remain unchanged, the varying element being the ending. In the flexion of personal pronouns however endings proper are hardly in evidence, and from case to case and number to number it is the stem itself which varies. From the view-point of number at least this is however as it should be, for here the conception of duality or plurality is altogether different from that of nouns or generic pronouns. If *áśvaḥ* = horse, *áśvau* = hore + horse. But similar equations cannot be applied to personal pronouns ; *áham* = I, but *āvā́m* = I + you or I + he, never I + I ! There is therefore nothing to wonder at if altogether different stems are used in the inflexion of the personal pronouns.

Another chief characteristic of the pronominal flexion is to be found in the liberal use of the particle *-am*, which plays no unimportant part also in the nominal flexion as shown above. It is in evidence even in *tvám* and *ahám*. The cognate languages clearly show that the Indo-European word for "you" was **tu-*: cf. Greek *tu* (Doric), Lat. *tū*, etc. This *tu* (= you) may be still found in Ṛgvedic passages like *ā́ tū́ gahi prá tú drava* (8, 13, 14). The particle *tu* in the Gāθās of Avesta may everywhere be taken to mean "you", and its regular enclitic position renders support to the view that it is nothing but the original Indo-European pronoun. The particle *-am* (<*Indo-European *-om*) had been attached to it however at least as early as the Indo-Iranian period, cf. Avestan *tvəm*. In the case of *áham* this particle had been attached to the original stem **eĝh-*[1] already in the Indo-European period, as is proved by Lat. *egom-et*. Yet the form *ego* (= Gr. *egṓ*) of the same language shows that the nasal element in it was not indispensable. The stem in its naked form *eĝ(h)-* is clearly seen in Lith. *eš*, Arm. *es* etc. In acc. sg. the forms *tvā́m mā́m* have their exact parallels in Avestan and Old Persian. The final nasal of these forms is not the accusative ending; it is due to their contraction with the particle *-am* as is proved by the enclitic forms *tvā mā*. In instr. sg. the RV. knows beside classical *tváyā* also *tvā́*, which is, of course, *tu* + *ā́*. Avestan instr. *θwā* proves

1 The exact nature of the consonant element cannot be determined. Had it been aspirated the Greek form too should have retained the aspiration. Had it been unaspirated there should have been no aspiration in Skt.

the antiquity of this form ; *tvàyā*, like *mā́yā* (beside which no *mā́* in instr. can be proved to have existed in Skt.), is of later origin. It is, in fact, a case of double ending, like *devā́saḥ* or *pṛtsuṣu*. The form *tvā́* (from **tu-*) in instr. sg. itself came to be regarded as stem later, and, like feminine *ā*-stems, gave rise to the form in *-ayā*. In dative the forms in classical Skt. are *túbhyam*, *màhyam*. These are known also in RV., but, on the evidence of metre, they have often to be read as *túbhya*, *màhya*. As the Avesta knows only these nasalless forms they must be the older ones. The corresponding Latin forms too (*tibi*, *mihi*) know no nasal. The abl. singulars *màt*, *tvàt* have their exact parallels in Avestan *maṯ*, *θwaṯ*. The form *mámat* (RV.) is evidently due to contamination of *mát* and *máma*. Of *tàva* and *máma* in gen. the former is of Indo-European antiquity, cf. Avestan *tava*, Gr. *teós* etc., but of the latter neither of the two *m* is certain, for the corresponding Avestan and O. Ch. Sl. forms are *mana* and *mene* respectively, and the corresponding Armenian form *im* renders even the initial *m* uncertain. In loc. sg. *máyi* is well attested in RV., but not so *tváyi*, for which is mostly found *tvé*. The relation between *tvé* and *tvàyi* might be the same as between *ádhvan* and *àdhvani*.

In dual, just as in nominal flexion, the number of specific forms is greatly restricted. Yet, even with reference to those few forms, much discrepancy is found between the Vedic and the classical language. The tendency of the latter has been to progressively substitute forms of pronouncedly dual type. Thus the older *yuvàbhyām āvàbhyām* were gradually supplanted by *yuvā́bhyām āvā́bhyām*. Similarly, *yuvā́m āvā́m* are confined to accusative dual only in the oldest texts, the corresponding forms in nominative being *yuvám āvám*. But already in the later Vedic period the *am*-forms have been completely supplanted by those in *-ām* also in nominative.

In nom. pl. these pronouns take the forms *vayám yūy-ám*, in both of which the element *-am*, so much in evidence in pronominal flexion, is a later accretion, as is proved by Goth. *vei-s* and *ju-s*. To judge by the corresponding Avestan form *yūžəm* of the latter, it ought to have been **yūram* in Skt. The form *yūyám* is clearly due to analogy with *vayám* in which the element *y* is of I.-E. antiquity (cf. Goth. *vei-s*). In all the oblique cases the forms in plural are characterised by an infixed *-sm-*, cf. *asmā́n yuṣmā́n, asmát yuṣmát* etc. This *-sm-* is certainly of Indo-European origin, cf. Avestan *ahma*, Gr. *amme* etc. The same *-sm-* appears, also in the singular of other pronouns, cf. *ásmai ásmin, tásmai tásmin* etc., and there too it is derived from the original Indo-European, cf. Goth. *imma þamma* (*mm*<*sm*), Umbrian *esmei pusme* etc. Most astonishing of all are the forms in gen. pl. which are characterised not only by this *-sm-* but are further distinguished by the ending *-ākam* (*asmā́kam, yuṣmā́kam*). On the evidence of Avestan *ahmākəm, yušmakəm* they must be of Indo-Iranian antiquity, and they must be connected with the adjectives *asmā́ka yuṣmā́ka*. But it is yet unknown how they so early became the recognised pronominal forms in plural. The feminine counterpart of this ubiquitous *-sm-* is *-sy-* both in Skt. and Avestan, cf. Skt. *asyái* : Av. *ahyāi* etc. Further back this *-sy-* is met by *-ssi-* in Old Prussian (see Wackernagel, III. p. 505) and *-s-* in Germanic, cf. Goth. *þizai, þizōs*.

If any speculation as to the multiple stems of these personal pronouns is permissible, it may be said that they date from those early times when the thought-element common to such concepts as *I, me, we, us* had not yet been discovered by man, and which therefore had to be expressed by quite different stems. Other pronouns too show similar heteroclitic stems, but never to such an extent as *asmad-yuṣmad-*, e. g. *sáḥ : tám* (cf. Gr. *hó : tón*), or *i-m-ám : i-d-ám* (cf. Lat. *id*) from the stem *i-*.

SANSKRIT VERBAL SYSTEM.

Finite verb-forms in the original Indo-European were even more composite in character than the forms of noun or pronoun. They were indifferent to gender, but, *en revanche*, they had to express the various *modes* of action (which however later gradually assumed temporal values) and, to some extent, also time. Every finite verb-form in Sanskrit was in fact equivalent to a sentence of modern languages, for it defined not only the deed but the doer as well, and that with such precision that in most cases no separate mention of the doer was necessary at all, it being necessary, in fact, only in the third person. This seems to reflect that very early state of human mind when mankind had not yet learnt to think of the doer and the deed separately, when the function of the forms concerned was merely to express the accomplished fact of a deed without analysing it, and which, therefore could dispense with a separate hint as to the doer. Even in the historical period most languages, including Sanskrit, retained an important group of impersonal verbs, chiefly expressing various meteorological phenomena or bodily pain or pleasure. But it is open to question whether all of these impersonalia are derived from the original stock of the basic Indo-European language. Some verbs may be proved to have become impersonal only in the historical period due to various causes. From the available data however it cannot be proved that the impersonal use of these verbs was the only one known in the original Indo-European.

A typical composite Sanskrit verb-form may consist of an augment, a reduplication syllable, the root, a connecting vowel and the ending, as in *á-ja-grabh-a-m* (from root *grabh-*). The first element *a-* of this form is the so-called augment prefixed to verb-forms to indicate that the action in question had taken place in the past. It is of Indo-European origin, for it is employed for the same purpose and in the same way also in Avestan, Greek and Armenian, and on the strength of a sole doubtful form (Goth. *iddja* : O. Engl. *eode*) it is sometimes claimed also for Germanic.

The facultative use of the augment in Vedic, Avestan and Greek even in those cases where it is considered indispensable in classical Sanskrit, shows that the augment was not an integral part of the verb-forms concerned, but simply a preverb. This is proved clearly by the fact that the augment obeys the same laws of accent as other preverbs both in Sanskrit and Greek. Of several preverbs prefixed to a finite verb-form usually only the last gets the accent in Sanskrit. Now, the augment, which is placed immediatety before the stem, always takes the accent upon itself leaving bare the other preverbs preceding it. It is clear that this could take place only because the augment itself was a preverb.* Precisely the same conditions may be observed also in Greek, in which language likewise the accent of compound verbs was not allowed to go beyond the first preverb. In fact here too, in augment-tenses, the accent stays on the augment and cannot travel further beyond.

According to the unanimous testimony of Sanskrit and Greek, therefore, the augment was originally an independent

* For had it been an integral part of the verb-form itself there is no reason why the preverb preceding the augment should not be accented instead.

preverb. Various anomalies in the sandhi of this augment further strengthen this view, for they show that the augment was still considered to be so foreign to the verb-form it preceded that even the usual rules of internal sandhi could not be applied to it. From the roots *iṣ-* and *ud-* the augmented forms in imperfect ought to have been **écchat* (<*á + icchat*) and ** ónat* (<*á + unat*) respectively, but we find instead *aicchat* and *aúnat*. The initial diphthongs of these forms can be explained only if it is assumed that the augment had succeeded in preserving its independence. Nor is it an accident that these apparent diphthongs have sometimes even a dissyllabic value in RV. and are actually to be read as *aï*, *aü* (see above, p. 63). A more eloquent proof of the complete autonomy once enjoyed by the so-called augment can be hardly imagined.

The augment sometimes appears as long in RV. before a semi-vowel,—mostly before *v* (Whitney § 585 a). The redactors of the Ṛgvedic text considered this long augment to be nothing but the usual short one extended under exigencies of metre. In the Padapāṭha therefore, with one exception, in all these forms this long augment is read as short. Yet, similar conditions prevailing in Greek (see Brugmann-Thumb, p. 308) show that even though the long augment might have been originally identical with the short one, it was in existence already in the Indo-European epoch.

Next to the augment comes the reduplication-syllable *-ja-* in the verb-form taken as model. The mechanical and morphological aspects of present and perfect reduplication have been already discussed in chapter II in connection with Avestan. Here, on the contrary, we are concerned mainly with reduplication as a vital factor in the general principles of verbal flexion. Yet it will be necessary to define with greater precision the various types of verbal reduplication and some allied problems.

Like the augment the reduplication-syllable too seems to have once been but loosely connected with the stem it preceded. For the initial sounds of some Greek roots are observed to undergo the same change after the reduplication syllable as are normally expected only in absolute initial. Moreover it is possible to show that in the original Indo-European there was no loss of aspiration in the reduplication-syllable of roots with an initial aspirate,—which could be possible, evidently, only because the reduplication-syllable was regarded as something separate from the verb-form in question. Thus *e.g.* the Greek form *pépheuge* (from I.-E. **bheuĝ-*) cannot be explained phonologically unless it is assumed that the law of dissimilation of aspirates had not worked in its case, for otherwise it would have become **bepheuge* <**bhebheuge*.

Moreover, reduplication is not of the same kind everywhere,—various types of verbal reduplication may be proved to have existed already in the Indo-European period. In the so-called intensive reduplication actually the whole of the root is repeated, cf. *jar-bhuri-ti*, Gr. *por-phū́r-ō* etc. It is a peculiar feature of this reduplication that in the reduplication-syllable an original *r* is sometimes changed into a nasal through dissimilation, cf. *cañ-cūrya-te*, *cañ-cal-a**. Even these apparently anomalous cases of intensive reduplication are derived from the original Indo-European, for in analogous cases in Greek the same dissimilation of *r* into *n*

* From root *car-* ; *l* is here equivalent to *r*.

may be observed, cf. *gag-galízō, den-drúō* etc. (Bgmn.-Th. p. 303). Most remarkable of all are perhaps the instances of the so-called Attic reduplication found, apart from Sanskrit, also in Greek and Armenian. Five roots beginning with prosodically long *a*, reduplicate not with *a-*, but with the syllable *ān-*, e.g. *ān-áṃś-a* (from *aṃś-*) and *ān-aj-é* (from *añj-*). Beginning from these roots containing a nasal, *ān-* became the reduplication syllable also of other roots without any inherent nasal, thus *ān-ṛc-úḥ* from *arc-* and *ān-ṛh-úḥ* from *arh-*. Precisely this kind of reduplication may be observed also in Greek, where however the reduplication-syllable is not always characterised by a nasal as in Sanskrit, cf. *ed-ēdṓs* : Skt. *ā́da*, *or-ṓra* : Skt. *ā́ra*. The very common perfect form *ak-ḗkoa* from *akoú-ō* is the most familiar example of Attic reduplication in Greek. For Sanskrit however it remains still to know why only nasal roots were primarily affected by this Attic reduplication, which gradually spread contagion also to other roots without any nasal.

In every grammar of classical Sanskrit reduplication is regarded as an anomaly of verbal flexion. Reduplicating roots have been classed together by all ancient Indian grammarians, but that only from a mechanical point of view. None of them has ever tried to show why particular roots *have* to reduplicate and others not. Ancient Greek grammarians were equally unsuccessful in this respect in the exposition of their language. It is one of the most remarkable achievements of the modern science of comparative grammar to discover the *principle* of reduplication in verbal flexion.

The principle of reduplication may be most conveniently demonstrated by means of the two forms *ábhāt* (from *bhā-*)

and *ásthat* (from *stha-*). Both these forms are exactly of the same type, and yet *ábhāt* is imperfect and *ásthat* is aorist.

An indication as to the cause of this apparent anomaly will be found if their respective present-stems are compared. The present-stem of *bhā-* is the root itself, but that of *sthā-* is the reduplicated stem *tiṣṭha-*. *Sthā-* is by no means an isolated root in this respect, for root-aorists as a rule show reduplicated stems in present. Nothing can be farther from the truth than to say that only roots with a reduplicating present-stem are capable of forming root-aorists, yet, as Whitney (§ 830) has observed, the roots which are decidedly the most frequent and conspicuous representatives of this formation are all, excepting one, roots with a reduplicating present-stem, namely *gā-* (*jigāti*), *dā-*, *dhā-*, *pā-** (*píbati*), *sthā-* and *bhū-*. Exactly the same condition prevails also in Greek, for here too the verbs forming a root-aorist are precisely those which by preference exhibit a reduplicated present (Hirt, Griech. Laut- u. Formenlehre, § 424 b), e. g. *dí-dō-mi* : *é-dō-ka*, *ti-thē-mi* : *é-thē-ka*, *hí-stē-mi* : *é-stē-n* etc. This can be hardly a fortuitous coincidence. It has to be admitted therefore that verbs forming root-aorists are precisely those which exhibit a reduplicated stem in present, and *vice versa*, and that there is an organic relation between root-aorists and reduplicating presents. And it further shows that the true relation between aorists and presents is quite different from what it is represented to be by classical grammarians. The aorist is nothing but a kind of present. In fact, all stems of the

* It is important to note in this connection that the homonymous root *pā-* "to protect" with a nonreduplicating present (*pāti*) has no root-aorist.

present-system can be broadly divided into two categories: (i) present-present, and (ii) present-aorist. Judging by the state of things in classical Greek, the present-present would be equivalent to English present-continuous, *e.g. is going, is coming,* etc., whereas present-aorist would correspond to simple present in English, *e.g. goes, comes,* etc. In translating from English into Greek we have therefore to use the imperfect to render the continuous past (*égraphe*=was writing), but to indicate the simple past the aorist has to be used (*égrapsa*=he wrote). But classical Greek does not represent the original state of things in this respect. That was rather just the opposite of what we find in classical Greek! Of all the various nuances associated with the aorist-stem that of *effectuation* seems to have been most prominent originally. But it was a timeless effectuation, without any consideration of past, present or future. "The contrast between the present and the aorist is without doubt one of those peculiarities of Indo-European verbs which proved to be of the greatest importance for the ulterior development of verbal flexion" (Meillet).

The contrast between present and aorist is primarily semasiological, and not morphological. This is proved *inter alia* by the fact that present and aorist conveying the *same* sense often take recourse to *different* roots, one durative (present-present) and the other expressing an action pure and simple without any consideration or duration (present-aorist). Thus the durative root Skt. *ád-mi*: Gr. *éd-menai* knows only forms of present, but its aorist is furnished by the root *ghas-*, cf. Skt. *á-ghaḥ*: Gr. *é-phage*. Similarly the root *as-* (durative) has a present but no aorist, which has therefore to be supplied by the aoristic root *bhū-*, cf. *á-bha-t*. Root-suppletion in the verbal flexion of Skt. and other Indo-European languages is in fact primarily due to this basic distinction between present and aorist; cf. further *paś-* (only present) : *dṛś-* (aorist, as well as future and perfect), *brū-* (only present) : *vac-* (aorist, future, perfect), *han-* (present, future, perfect) : *vadh-* (only aorist). Future and perfect are but particular nuances of the present, and as the aorist is a type of present so far as the temporal quality is concerned, there is nothing to wonder at if the aorist would have at its side sometimes also a future and a perfect. This shows that the first principle according to which the Indo-European verbal stems are to be classified is the so-called *aspect* of action (*Aktionsart* in German is a more expressive term). In Pāṇinian grammar the aorist has become a simple *tense* of the *past*. But originally the aorist had nothing to do with tense, and a past sense could be expressed by means of an aorist-stem only if it was supported by the augment. It was as good a present as the present itself. Taking for granted that all Indo-European verbal roots primarily expressed actions and processes of the present, the roots expressing processes—going, seeing—would be called present roots, and those primarily expressing not the process but the action—reaching, finding—would be called aorist roots (see above p. 20). The difference is here neither temporal nor modal,—it lies only in the aspect of action.

If the correlation between aorist and present is truly as it has been represented above, there is no reason why it should come to light only in the case of root-aorists and reduplicating presents. But that is not the case either. In fact in a series of present formations corresponding pairs of aorist and present stems may be easily detected. It is too much to expect that complete sets on both sides could still be pointed out in all the languages. Yet, by comparing the different languages it is possible to discover the main outline of the original picture. But it has always to be borne in mind that the suppletive use of different roots was an essential feature of Indo-European verbal flexion. There is nothing to wonder at, therefore, if we often miss an aorist at the side of a present, and *vice versa*.

On the whole the aorist stems show much less variety of formation than the present stems. It is therefore commonly held that when two similar verb-forms are found side by side, one with a stem-suffix and the other without any, the latter should be regarded as an aorist-form, and the former as a form of the present. Thus from the root *kṛ-* the form *ákṛṇot* is imperfect, but *ákar*[1], which is formantically the same form *minus* the radical suffix *-nu-*, is aorist. Similarly *ágaccham* from *gam-*, with the radical suffix *-sko-* (see below), is present, but the same form without this suffix—*ágamam*—is aorist. In imperative too, *su-nó-tu* is present, but *só-tu* is aorist. With regard to the personal endings however the difference is as clear as it can be desired : the present stem may take both primary and secondary endings, but the aorist stem takes only the secondary ones. The aorist stem cannot take the primary ending even when it is unaugmented. As shown above, *ákar(t)*, *ágamam*, with secondary endings, are true aorist forms. Without the augment they would give rise to the so-called injunctive forms *kár(t)*, *gamám*. But aorist forms with

1. For **ákart*, Sanskrit retaining only the first consonant of a compound at the end of a word.

primary endings such as **kár-mi* or **gán-mi* are quite impossible.*

Next to the reduplicating presents the most characteristic present stems are perhaps those with the inchoative suffix *-*sk̂(h)o*-, such as *gaccha-*, *pṛccha-*, *yaccha-* from *gam-*, *praś-*, *yam-*. Like the reduplicating presents these inchoative presents too often form root aorists, *e.g.* *ágamam* from *gam-* and (*á*)*yamam* from *yam-*. Analogous conditions prevailing in Greek prove that this correlation between inchoative presents and root-aorists is a relic of the original Indo-European, cf. *báskō* : *ébēn*, *gignṓskō* : *égnōn*, *pháskō* *éphēn*, etc. This inchoative radical suffix became very productive in Latin and Germanic, but in Sanskrit it remained confined to a few roots only.

Thurneysen has proved for Greek that all roots ending in *g*, which form an *s*- aorist, must have a present in *-numi*, *e.g.* *meíg-nu-mi* : *é-meix-a*, *zeúg-nu-mi* : *é-zeux-a*, *plḗg-nu-mi* : *é-plēx-a* etc. Similarly all Greek verbs forming a present in *-nnumi* (<*-snumi*) have necessarily an *s*-aorist, *e.g.* *sbé-nnumi* : *é-sbe-s-a*, *kerá-nnumi* : *e-kéras-a*. Nasal presents and sigmatic aorists in Greek are therefore similar correlatives as root-aorists and reduplicating presents. It can be hardly an accident that precisely the most characteristic verbs of the nasal classes in Sanaskrit exhibit sigmatic aorists : *kṛ-ṇó-ti* : *á-kār-ṣ-īt* ; *ci-nó-ti* : *a-cai-ṣ-am*, *cay-iṣ-ṭam* ; *dhū-nó-ti* : *á-dhū-ṣ-a-ta* ; *śṛ-ṇó-mi* : *á-śrau-ṣ-īt*, etc. Yet both the nasal presents and sigmatic aorists are of so various types that for practical purposes it will be best to describe them separately and point out their Indo-European affinities in each case.

---

* Excepting in subjunctive, about which further below.

The three chief types of nasal presents recognised by ancient Indian grammarians - the 5th, 7th and 9th root classes - are derived from the original Indo-European. The same is true also of the roots of the sub-group *mucādi* (*mu-ñ-c-á-ti*).

That the nasal element is actually an 'infix' in forms like *yu-ná-k-ti* is proved beyond doubt by the allied forms *yu-yója, yu-yujé* etc., in which there is no trace of the nasal. In forms like *śṛṇómi* etc. the nasal element has become apparently more closely identified with the original root, for here it is the nasal syllable (*-nu-*) which is strengthened (*-nó-*) in the present-stem. Yet the aorist forms *á-śro-t, śru-dhí* at once reveal its real character. Sometimes allied languages render help in finding out the original form of the root concerned. Thus the Indo-European base **stereu̯-* has on the one hand given rise to Goth. *strau-ja* (<**streu̯-*), and on the other to Sanskrit *stṛṇó-mi, stṛṇu-máḥ* (<**stṛ-neu̯-*, **stṛ-nu-*).

In the two latter Sanskrit forms *-neu-* : *-nu-* has difinitely become a radical suffix ; but the imported element here is only *n*, for, on the evidence of Goth. *strau-ja, eu* : *u* must have been present there already at a still earlier time. The infixed nasal, combined with the older *eu* : *u*, gave rise to the new radical suffix *neu* : *nu* which is in evidence in *ṛ-ṇó-mi* : *ṛ-ṇu-máḥ, śak-nó-ti* : *śak-nu-táḥ*, etc. (Root class V, cf. Gr. *ór-nu-mi*). The same infixed nasal combining with an original *ā* gave rise to the nasal infix *nā*. Thus the root *jyā-*, i.e. *jiā-* (cf. *ji-jyaú*), strengthened by this nasal became *jinā-*, hence *jinā́ti* etc. Gradually *nā* became an independent radical suffix and was freely combined with roots which had never contained an *ā*, *e.g.*

krī-ṇā́-ti (Root-class IX, Gr. *dam-nā́-mi*). The eighth root-class of the ancient Indian grammarians is a nasal-present only in appearance. That the nasal element in them is no 'infix' at all, but part of the roots themselves is proved by the fact that all the old representatives of this type, namely *kṣan-*, *tan-*, *man-*, *van-* and *san-*, retain this nasal also in the aorist (cf. *kṣaniṣṭhāḥ*, *atan*, *amaṃsta*, *vámsat*, and *asāniṣam*). In fact the basis *tano-* in *tanóti* is not derived from Indo-European *teneu̯-* as might be ordinarily expected : it is in reality nothing but *tn̥-no-* as Brugmann ingeniously suggested, thus showing that formantically this class is identical with the Root-class V (*r̥-ṇó-mi*). As the result of this formal coincidence of these two types one of the most important roots of class V was analogically transferred to class VIII : *kr̥-ṇó-mi* became *kar-ó-mi* on the analogy of *tanómi* etc.

All these various nasal presents are characterised by a mobile nasal element variously placed, sometimes strengthened by different vowels. Now the question arises, was this *n* from origin an independent formative element or was it the weakened form of a fuller particle *ne/no*. A comparison of verbs of Class VII (*rudh-* etc.) with those of *muc*-class points to the second of these two probabilities. The two forms *yunák-ti* and *muñcá-ti*, for example, may at first sight appear to be very dissimilar. Yet their plurals are of identical formation—*yuñján-ti* and *muñcán-ti* ; and allowing for the fact that *yunák-ti* is an athematic form and *muñcá-ti* is thematic, there remains nothing in the way of equating them excepting that in the former the nasal infix is *na* and in the latter it is merely *n*. This apparent discrepancy, again, is fully explained by the place of accent, which, as usual, was shifted to the thematic vowel in the thematic form *muñc-á-ti*, but remained on the present-suffix *na* in the athematic *yunák-ti*. *Yunák-ti* and *muñcá-ti* are therefore identical formations, and we are thus forced to two different conclusions : firstly, that the roots of Class VII (*rudh-* etc.) are nothing but the athematic counterparts of roots of the *muc*-Class, and secondly that the original aspect of the nasal infix was *ne/no* and not merely *n*. For if the *n* of the *muc*-Class and *ne/no* of the *rudh*-Class are organically connected with each other, the most rational hypothesis as to their inter-relation would be to assume that *n* is nothing but the unaccented weakened form of *ne/no*. The origin of this *ne/no* however still remains as obscure as ever.

The *s* of the sigmatic aorists is singularly like the *n* of the nasal presents. Combining variously with various other formantic elements it laid the foundation of four distinct types of aorist-stems, e. g. (i) *s*-aorist, (ii) *iṣ*-aorist, (iii) *siṣ*-aorist and (iv) *sa*-aorist. Besides these sigmatic aorists there are further (v) the *a*-aorist and (vi) the reduplicating aorist in Sanskrit.

If it is borne in mind that, augment apart, formantically there need be no difference between present and aorist forms excepting that the former can take both primary and secondary endings but the latter only the secondary ones, the most difficult and indistinct of the aorist formations, namely the *a*-aorist, becomes at once the easiest to explain. For the *a*-aorists, on this hypothesis, may be explained simply as unaugmented forms with secondary endings of roots taking the suffix *a* in present. In fact, according to Whitney's list (Roots, p. 223) of the sixty roots forming *a*-aorist, no less than forty belong to those present classes which are actually characterised by the suffix -(*y*)*a*-, namely, root-classes I, IV and VI. Starting from these roots *a*-aorists came to be formed analogically also from roots like *khyā*-, *vyā*-, etc., e.g. *ákhya-t*, *á-vya-t*, etc. The *a*-aorist has its exact counterpart in Greek *é-lip-on* (from *leípō*) etc.

The same hypothesis suffices to explain also the *s*-aorists of the type *ábhār-ṣ-am* from *bhṛ*-. The *s*-aorists presuppose *s*-presents just as *a*-aorists presuppose *a*-presents as shown above, and Brugmann (Griechische Grammatik §376) aptly remarks that the *s*-aorist may be regarded as the preterite of an *s*-present. But *s*-presents are unknown in Sanskrit (yet see Bartholomae, Vorgeschichte § 136) except in roots forming *ya*-presents. This -*s*- combined with the suffixal -*ya*- early gave rise to the suffix -*sya*- which became the symbol of future tense in Sanskrit.

The suffix -*sya*- is not peculiar to Sanskrit alone, as might be assumed from its limited use in the older language and gradual increase later. (Only sixteen roots form *sya*-stem in the RV). It is well attested in Iranian, cf. Avestan *vax-šyā* : Skt. *vak-ṣyá-mi*, and Lithuanian forms like *lìk-siu*, which corresponds to Skt. *rek-ṣyá-ti* root (*ric*-), prove its existence in still earlier times. What is peculiar to Sanskrit is the absence of the radical suffix -*sa*- with a similar function. But its existence is very much in evidence in Greek and Latin, cf. Gr. *leípsō*: *leípō*, Lat. *dīxō*: *dīcō*. and there are clear traces of it also in Prākrit, cf. *dāhāmi*, *dāhāmo* from root *dā*- (Pischel § 530). Sanskrit *s*-aorists are to be directly connected with these sigmatic forms, which were originally simply desiderative presents, and had nothing to do with future tense.

Once an explanation of *s*-aorists (type *á-bhār-ṣ-am*) has been found, that of *sa*-aorists ceases to be a separate problem at all, for *sa*-aorists are nothing but thematic *s*-aorists (see Brugmann-Thumb § 381). It is a peculiar feature of the *sa*-aorists that all the roots showing this form have in final *j*, *ś*, *ṣ*, or *h*,—every one of which would phonetically give rise to *-kṣa-* when combind with the *-sa-* of the suffix. Only nine roots form the *sa*-aorist in the Saṃhitās (MacDonell § 535), *e.g.* *mṛj-*: *mṛkṣatam*, *spṛś-*: *áspṛkṣat*, *dviṣ-*: *dvikṣat*, *ruh-*: *árukṣat*, etc.

The *iṣ*-aorists of Sanskrit at the side of *s*-aorists cannot fail to remind one of the *iṣya*-futures (*kar-i-ṣyá-ti*) at the side of *sya*-forms (*drak-ṣyá-ti*). In fact, *iṣ*-aorists are nothing but *seṭ* forms of *s*-aorists. They may be therefore described also as *s*-aorists of the so-called dissyllabic roots, cf. *á-stariṣ-am* from *star-* (Brugmann-Thumb, p. 363). Strictly speaking, it is inaccurate to make a separate category out of *iṣ*-aorists as distinct from *s*-aorists, for in that case there can be no reason why a separate category of *iṣya*-futures should not be recognised at the side of those in *-sya*. The *iṣ*-aorist is well attested both in Iranian (Bartholomae, Vorgeschichte § 157) and Greek (Brugm. Ibid.).

Most difficult to explain among all the sigmatic aorists of Sanskrit are those characterised by the suffix *-siṣ-*. They are extremely rare, there being altogether less than twenty forms from seven roots. The Avesta knows only a single form of *sis*-aorist (Barth. § 158), and no sure trace of it can be found in Greek (see however Brugmann-Thumb § 381, f.-n. 2). Very probably this formation is due to early crossing of *s*-aorists with *iṣ*-aorists.

Only the reduplicating (asigmatic) aorists of the type

ájījanat from *jan-* now still remain to be explained. A reduplicating stem in aorist is indeed surprising, for it has been shown above that aorists as a rule have simpler stems than the present forms, and particularly the reduplicating presents show, not reduplicating aorists as might be expected, but root-aorists. Yet, strictly speaking, there is nothing out of the ordinary in this formation excepting its meaning, which is almost always *causative*. From a purely formantic point of view this aorist may be regarded as an augment-tense of the reduplicating present with secondary endings (see Bartholomae, Vorgeschichte § 127). Or it may be connected with reduplicating perfect stems. Most of the roots forming reduplicating aorists follow indeed the rule of present-reduplication (with *i*, *u* in the reduplication syllable). Yet forms showing perfect-reduplication (with *a* in the reduplication syllable) are not rare, cf. *a-da-dhāv-at*. Besides Sanskrit the reduplicating aorist is known in Avestan (*e.g.* *zīzanaṯ*) but nowhere else.

Lastly, a separate mention should be made of the verbal suffix *-ya-* (of root-class IV) which is of great importance for Skt. in more ways than one. It is of Indo-European origin, cf. *páś-ya-ti* : Avestan *spas-yeiti*, Latin *spec-io* ; *pácya-te* : Gr. *péssō* (<**peqᵘi̯ō*). Yet the fact that no *ya*-aorist as distinct from *a*-aorist had ever existed in Sanskrit seems to suggest that at an early date *-ya-* came to be regarded as a secondary form derived from the older suffix *-a-*. A good number of roots (e.g. *tan-*, *tṛṣ-*, *das-*, *radh-*, etc.) forming both *a-* and *ya*-presents might be adduced in support of this view. Gradually this suffix however became the symbol of passive-stem in Sanskrit. The connecting link between act. *páś-ya-ti* and pass. *dṛś-yá-te* is doubtless to be sought in the intransitives with suffix *-ya-* such as *tuṣ-yá-ti*, and it is a significant fact that most of the verbs of this group are actually intransitive (MacDonell § 437). In classical Sanskrit these intransitives as a rule take medial endings, but in the older language active endings are also allowed, cf. Ved. *jī́ryati* but class. *jīryate* (Thumb, Handbuch, § 381). The accent on the root-syllable in *jī́ryati* may seem to go against the theory that *ya*-passives are derived from *ya*-presents. Yet the weak form of the syllable under accent clearly shows that it is here secondary. As Bartholomae has tersely put it, the original accent on the thematic vowel has been preserved in Sanskrit only in those forms which were used as passives, while in all others it was thrown back upon the radical syllable (Vorgeschichte § 148).

Hitherto we have discussed the principal present and aorist stem-types of Sanskrit occurring in the indicative mood only. Theoretically all these stem-types should occur also in the other moods, namely subjunctive, injunctive, optative (including precative or benedictive) and imperative. This is however not the case, for none of these other moods may even be compared to indicative in the richness of forms and general importance for the language. Formantically too, the different modal stems may be regarded as simple variants of the indicative stem,—the imperative stem is even identical with it. The same is the case also with the injunctive, which has no distinctive stem-sign at all, for forms of all the augment-tenses (imperfect, aorist, pluperfect), shorn of the augment, may serve as injunctive. We are therefore concerned here, apart from indicative, mainly with the subjunctive and the optative.

The indicative is the mood of simple statement by which no subjective inclination or expectation on the part of the speaker is conveyed. The subjunctive on the other hand is the mood of expectation, and formantically its modal stem is characterised by the suffix *-a* added to that of the indicative. Thus *śṛṇáv-a-d vácāṃsi me* signifies "may he hear my words". This modal suffix is quite distinct in the case of athematic verbs : *ás-ti* in indicative but *ás-a-t(i)* is subjunctive. It is of Indo-European origin, for subjunctives of other languages too are characterised by the same modal suffix. Thus to Skt. *á-s-a-t* corresponds Latin *er-i-t* (*r* and *i* of the latter are exact phonetic counterparts of *s* and *a* of the former). But in Latin these forms came to be used in future at a very early date. In the case of thematic verbs this modal suffix combines with the thematic vowel : *bhár-a-ti* (ind.) *bhár-ā-ti* (subj.). The same contraction of the thematic vowel with the modal suffix may be observed also in Greek, cf. *lú-o-mai* (ind.) : *lú-ō-mai* (subj.). Some Ṛgvedic subjunctive forms with dissyllabic *-ā-* prove however that the amalgamation of the modal suffix with the thematic vowel had not yet been fully achieved (see above, p. 64).

Theoretically, everyone of the present-stems described above, both of present and aorist, should have a corresponding subjunctive form, but such forms are not very common. There is only a single future form of the subjunctive mood, namely *kariṣyā́ḥ* from *kṛ-*. Perfect forms of this mood are quite rare, cf. *tatán-a-t(i)* from *tan-*. Subjunctive forms of aorists too, though rare, are not altogether wanting, cf. *néṣ-a-t (i)* from *nī-*.

The two distinct semantic values of the optative have

been clearly defined by Meillet (p. 189-90). Firstly, it may indicate something *possible* as opposed to a definite reality which is expressed by the indicative, and secondly it may be used to express a definite *desire*. Thus "*viśé ca kṣatrā́ya ca samádaṃ kuryām*" signifies "may I succeed in creating enmity between the people and the nobility", and *dámpatī aśnīyātām* signifies "husband and wife might eat". The modal suffix of the optative is *-yā*, which however becomes *-ī* (<i̯ə) in weak forms (cf. *dad-yā́-t* : *dad-ī-tá*). The same modal suffix with identical weakening in unstressed position is encountered also in other languages, cf. Lat. *s-iē-s* : *s-ī-mus*. In the case of thematic roots however the optative is throughout characterised by *i*. Combined with the thematic vowel *o* it formed the typical optative suffix *-oi-* in Greek, cf. Gr. *phéroi* etc. In Sanskrit this diphthong phonologically became *e*, cf. *bháret*. As a typical optative form of the *s*-aorist may be mentioned *di-ṣ-īyá* from *dā-*, with the radical vowel weakened to *i* (<ə). The so-called precative is a peculiar formation of Sanskrit which differs from the optative only in that its characteristic modal suffix is *-yās* : *-īs* and not *-yā* : *-ī*, and that it is formed almost exclusively from aorist-stems (see MacDonell §417).

Before discussing the personal endings it is necessary to discuss the formantic elements serving as a bridge between them and the stem. Two such links are used for this purpose, but both of them never occur in one and the same form. One is the thematic vowel, and the other the connecting vowel *-i* (*iṭ* of Sanskrit grammarians).

In *bháv-a-ti* from *bhū-*, for instance, the connecting vowel *a*, which connects the root with the ending, is called the thematic vowel. Very probably it is a relic from those early times when *roots* as such had not yet been abstracted out of congeneric forms as was done later by grammarians. The thematic stem is the crude form—Pāṇini's ***prātipadika***—which marks an intermediate stage between the roots, which are purely grammatical abstractions (inasmuch as no root as an independent element had ever existed in any language) and the grammatically constructed complete word-forms. Thus the form *bhava-* is presupposed both by *bhávati* and *bhavaná*. None of them necessarily presupposes the form *bhū-* (the root !) which owes its existence only to grammatical theory*. This crude-form need not necessarily end in a vowel as in *bhava-*; it might also end with a consonant, cf. *át-ti, an-ná* from *ad-*. If *ad-* in *átti* is called root, it follows logically that *bhava-* in *bhávati* should also get the same designation, Yet, in common usage, this practice is not followed. The *a*-form is never called the root. On the contrary it is said of the roots showing this *a*-form that they have been extended by the thematic vowel *-a*. Thus the stem *bhava-* is considered to be the root *bhū-* extended by the *thematic* vowel *a*. In consequence, roots of the type *ad-*, which take no such *-a*, are called *athematic.*

The testimony of Greek clearly shows that the original form of this connecting vowel was sometimes *e* and sometimes *o*, cf. *phér-e-te* : *phér-o-men*. As both these vowels have coincided in *a* in Sanskrit, no such qualitative difference in the thematic vowel may be observed in this language. As already mentioned in Chapters I and II, the personal endings too of the two types were partly different, but Sanskrit has generalised the thematic endings throughout the whole

* Forms like *ábhūt* do not necessarily prove the existence of a root *bhū-*, for it is nothing but the weakened form of * *á-bhav(a)t*.

system. In the thematic flexion, moreover, the accent was fixed and was never placed on the ending (unless of course the stem coalesced with it), *e.g. bhára-mi, bhára-maḥ* etc., but in athematic flexion the accent was free to move from stem to ending, cf. *é-mi* : *i-máḥ, cinó-mi* : *cinu-máḥ*.

The thematic vowel is thus a barrier which the accent cannot pass. Besides, it is a general characteristic of all verbal stems that the accent is normally placed in them on the suffix-element, cf. *e. g.* the nasal presents *kṛ-ṇó-ti, krī-ṇā́-ti*. Even when the accent is found to rest on the root-syllable it may be often proved to have been shifted there secondarily. The accentuation of *gácchati* for instance must have been different originally, for *ga-* (<*gṃ*) here is the reduced form of *gam-*. All this together strongly suggests that originally the place of accent in thematic forms was always on the thema-vowel.

The origin of the connecting vowel *-i-* is not different from that of the thema-vowel. Only in this case we have to imagine that the second syllable of the crude-form in question ended in a long vowel—*ē, ō* or *ā*.

The thema-vowel *-a* owes its origin, as we have seen, to the crude-form *bhava-* <Indo-European **bheue-*. But beside it there must have been in the original Indo-European another crude-form of the type **bheuē-*, with a long final vowel. Now, as two equally strong accents are impossible in one and the same word, the form **bheuē-* was often weakened to **bheuə-*,—whence Sanskrit *bhavi-* in *bhavi-ṣyá-ti bhavi-tā́ bhavi-túm* etc. Just as the final *-a* in *bhava-* came to be regarded as an extraneous element, in the same way the *-i* in *bhavi-* too received the status of an independent connecting link serving as a bridge between the root and the root-suffix,

which together form the stem. But unlike the thematic -*a*, the connecting vowel -*i*- does not connect the stem with the ending. It is therefore more closely associated with the root than the thema-vowel -*a*. The discovery of this connecting vowel -*i*- is rightly considered to be the greatest linguistic achievement of ancient Indian grammarians, though it was reserved for Ferdinand de Saussure to demonstrate its full significance for the history of Indo-European languages.

Lastly we have to discuss the personal endings of verbal flexion. They vary, firstly, according to the voices *active* and *middle*, and secondly according as they are *primary* or *secondary*. All these forms are shown, at least theoretically, by every number of every person. The perfect has moreover endings of its own. In the original Indo-European the endings varied also according as the stems were thematic or athematic, but in Sanskrit this distinction has been almost completely obiiterated. But it still shows some special endings peculiar to Imperative.

The primary endings as a rule have fuller forms than the secondary ones. Thus in 1. sg. the primary ending is -*mi*, but the corresponding secondary ending is only -*m* ; similarly in 2. sg. -*si* and -*s*, and in 3. sg. -*ti* and -*t*. As the secondary endings are usually associated with augment-tenses this difference in the forms of primary and secondary endings is not difficult to explain. As the stress was laid in the augment-tenses always on the augment, the personal endings in them, which are the farthest removed from it, were considerably weakened,—with the result that -*ti* became -*t*, -*mi* became -*m*, etc. This weakening had taken place already in the Indo-European period, for both sets of endings may be clearly observed also in other allied languages, particularly in Greek. Similarly in 3. pl. the primary ending is *-nti*, but the secondary one is *-nt*, cf. *bhára-nti*, *ábhara-n(t)*. In the case of athematic stems this ending often appears to be *-ati* as in 3. sg., cf. *dád-ati* in 3. pl. This *-ati* is however the regular phonetic representative of *-nti* after a consonant. In fact, *dád-ati* is derived from Indo-European **déd-n̥ti*. All the athematic roots do not however take the ending *-ati* in 3. pl., cf. *ád-anti*. These are evidently formed after thematic *bháranti* etc. The primary ending in 1. pl. is *-masi* (later *-mas*) which has its exact counterpart in Avestan *-mahi*. The Greek ending *-men* in this position is a later development, but cf. Doric *-mes*. The endings in dual are so different in the various languages that it is very difficult, and often impossible, to reconstruct their original forms.

The endings in perfect are altogether different, and that from the Indo-European epoch. In 1. sg. it is *-a*, cf. Sanskrit *véd-a* : Gr. *voīd-a*. Skt. shows the ending *-tha* in 2. person (*vét-tha*) to which corresponds *-tha* in Greek. But as Greek *-tha* may be derived from Indo-European *-dha*, the original form of this ending remains unknown. The most remarkable of all the endings in plural in Sanskrit is *-uḥ* (<*-ur*), e.g. *ja-gm-úḥ*, to which corresponds Avestan *-ərəš* and Latin *-ere* (*amav-ere*). That it is actually an *r*-ending, about which more below, had escaped the notice of ancient Indian grammarians. In the padapāṭha therefore the visarga resulting from this *r* is treated in the same way as that from *s*.

The endings in the middle are fuller than those of the active. Thus in sg. *-mai -sai -tai*, as opposed to *-mi -si -ti* in the active. They have of course become *-me*, *-se*, *-te* in Sanskrit, though in Greek they have retained their original forms. In 3. pl. the ending is as might be expected, i.e., *-ntai* in thematic forms (cf. *bhára-nte*) and *-ṇtai* in athematic ones (cf. *dád-ate*). In 1. pl. the endings are *-mahe* (primary) and *-mahi* (secondary) respectively in Sanskrit, corresponding to Avestan *-maide* and *-maidī*. In 2. pl. the primary ending in Indo-Iranian is *-dhvai*, whence Sanskrit *-dhve* Avestan *-duye*, and the corresponding secondary ending is *-dhvam* (= Avestan *-dūm*). The most remarkable of the secondary middle endings in Indo-Iranian is *-i* in 1. sg., cf. *á-kri* (from *kṛ-*), Avestan *aoj-i*. Combined with the thematic vowel it often gives rise to the ending *-e*, cf. *á-bhar-e*. In the optative however the corresponding ending is *-a*, cf. Sanskrit *bharey-a* Avestan *baray-a*. It is impossible to say whether this *-a* is derived from Indo-European *-m(i)*.

In imperative, the 2. sg. of thematic stems takes no ending at all, cf. *bhára* : Gr. *phére*, but the athematic ones may take the ending *-(d)hi*, cf. *i-hí* (<**i-dhí*) : Gr. *í-thi*, *vid-dhí* : Gr. *(v)ís-thi*. The ending *-tāt*, which, according to Pāṇini, replaces *-tu* and *-hi* when a benedictive sense is to be conveyed, is another characteristic feature of the imperative. This *-tāt* corresponds to Lat. *-tōt* (classical *-to*) and is therefore of Indo-European origin.

Lastly, we have to mention the mysterious *r*-endings which have been almost completely eliminated from classical Sanskrit. In the Vedic language these *r*-endings are extensively used in 3. pl. Beside the ending *-ur* in perfect mentioned above, an *r* is found also in the endings of imperative (*-ratām*, *-rām*, cf. *duh-rām*, *duh-ratām*), pluperfect (*-ram*, cf. *á-sa-sṛg-ram*), imperfect (*-ran*, cf. *a-duh-ran*, *á-śe-ran*) etc. The same element *-r-* in so many different places naturally raises the suspicion that it was originally impersonal in character. This is borne out by the Celtic languages in which the forms in *-ir, -ar, -er* are actually impersonal in value. Besides Italic and Celtic languages *r*-endings are used also in Tokharian, and this is a strong argument in favour of the Italo-Celtic affinity of Tokharian.